"Lynne beautifully shares ... ... personal experience and Biblical wisdom the practical action steps involved in the ongoing process of healing from sexual abuse, underlying the essential of moving away from victimhood and establishing identity in Jesus Christ. A must read for survivors at any stage in their healing journey."
—**Crystal Sutherland**, author of *Journey to Heal: Seven Essential Steps of Recovery for Survivors of Childhood Sexual Abuse* (Kregel Publications/2016)

"This is a masterpiece. It has made a difference to my life at a time when I've been under a lot of spiritual attack, helping me to focus on Jesus with concrete practical strategies and deep illustrations and stories from the gospels. This book will make a huge difference spiritually and emotionally for your readers."
—**Lauren Craft**, professional writer and journalist

"Lynne gracefully shares from the depths of her own experience and guides you on a path of restoration to wholeness. Along with the stories of women who have felt this despair, you'll realize you're not alone and there's hope at the end of a dark tunnel. *Unfolding* will be a resource you will share over and over."
—**Jessie Seneca**, author, speaker, and founder of More of Him Ministries

"For anyone who has been a victim and suffered in silence, felt guilty, ashamed, afraid…and longs for hope, healing and faith in God and man again, this book is definitely for you. Beautifully written yet real, raw and down-to-earth, *Unfolding* is full of candor, wisdom and truth."
—**Michele Chynoweth**, bestselling author

"Your experience, sharing others' words, and your research is so valuable. It isn't textbook, clichés, and pat answers. It's human and divine coming together and making a difference on this sin wrecked planet. I will definitely be recommending it to others."

—**Joetta Moyer**, missionary

"Thanks for sharing so openly and honestly to the world."

—**Hosanna Lo**, missionary

"Lynne conveys a story that will make you want to read on. It communicates truth with clarity and spiritual insight. Beautifully written, with a heart for those who need compassion, her knowledge, research, and experience will help bring healing to women broken by sexual intrusion."

—**Sherry Lynch**, teacher

"Unfolding is an insightful, sensitive, and practical resource for anyone suffering from sexual intrusion and abuse. It compassionately details how trust in a loving God will help ease the pain and transform the wounded self into something wholly beautiful."

—**Stephen Parker**, licensed psychologist, licensed professional counselor, author

May God's Spirit touch you with healing.
Ps 27:4 Lynne

Unfolding
Recovering Your Identity After Sexual Intrusion

LYNNE HEAD, LCMHC

This book reflects the author's present recollections of experiences over time. Some names and places have been changed, some events have been compressed, and some dialogue has been recreated.

A portion from the proceeds of this book will go to BraveWorks a ministry empowering women overcoming trauma and injustice.
https://www.braveworks.org

Copyright © Lynne Head, 2023

All rights reserved. Published by the Peppertree Press, LLC. The Peppertree Press and associated logos are trademarks of the Peppertree Press, LLC. No part of this publication may be reproduced, stored in a retrieval system, transmitted in any form or by any means, electronic, mechanical, photocopying, recording, or otherwise, without prior written permission of the publisher and author/illustrator.

Cover design by Jim Head.
Cover photo by Rachel Baughman.
Graphic design by Elizabeth Parry.

For information regarding permission, call 941-922-2662 or contact us at our website: www.peppertreepublishing.com or write to: The Peppertree Press, LLC. Attention: Publisher 715 N. Washington Blvd., Suite B Sarasota, Florida 34236

ISBN: 978-1-61493-886-6
Library of Congress: 2023908213
Printed: April 2023

Dedication

for Jana,
whom the Lord sent

for those who've known unspeakable sexual violence
who've experienced the slightest offense
and everyone in between—
may the healing balm of Gilead be yours

April 26, 2005
During
my daughter's
violin lesson,
I climbed a mountain path
in fresh pine air,
where dogwood flowers faded,
sunlight steamed on my back,
glittering rock crunched underfoot,
wind-tossed tree-shadows
danced on my path,
but through the din
of roofers hammering
and yapping dogs,
God spoke:
"I want you to write
your story."

Table of Contents

Introduction ix
CHAPTER 1 My Story 1

Part One: New Healing

CHAPTER 2 Why Is It So Hard To Talk About? 15
CHAPTER 3 Why Grieve Over Abuse? 23
CHAPTER 4 From Darkness into Light 35
CHAPTER 5 Why is Healthy Anger Necessary for Healing? 45

Part Two: New Identity

CHAPTER 6 Broken Dreams 59
CHAPTER 7 Grieving Lost Beauty 65
CHAPTER 8 Someone Better Suited 75
CHAPTER 9 Holding Onto Desire 87
CHAPTER 10 Is Jesus a Trustworthy Man? 95
CHAPTER 11 Little Girls in Adult Bodies 107
CHAPTER 12 Becoming a Daughter 119

Part Three: New Power

CHAPTER 13 Triggers and Trauma 127
CHAPTER 14 Learning Assertiveness 139
CHAPTER 15 When the Enemy Attacks 151

Part Four: New Freedom

CHAPTER 16 Finding Forgiveness 159

CHAPTER 17 Transforming Shame........................171

CHAPTER 18 Developing Closeness......................181

CHAPTER 19 Longing for A Safe Place....................185

Acknowledgements 191

Appendix 1: Tools of Expression and Communication ...195

Appendix 2: Hotline and Resources 203

Poems 205

References..274

Introduction

Women in every culture and time have endured sexual intrusion at varying levels of severity. As I write the account of my story, I struggle to share it since I know many women have endured more severe abuse than me. When I was molested, I was trapped and unable to escape my offender for nearly thirty hours. And once I went back to look at the span of my life, I realized there were a handful of other events that I would call abuse. I want to speak to women who, like me, may have had a one-time experience they dismissed, or situations which they questioned as to whether or not they were abusive.

Whether your experience comes from a date that went wrong, workplace harassment, or a stranger catcalling, when you put all the factors together, the accumulative effect of any unwanted sexual intrusion brings trauma to your mind, body, and soul.

For women who know the insufferable pain of ongoing childhood sexual abuse, adult abuse, prostitution, or trafficking, it's my prayer that you experience even greater healing than I have known. Listen to the courageous words of Joy, a friend of mine:

> At the age of three, I endured horrific and traumatic sexual abuse. My brain buried it deep until six years ago, when like a flood, all the memories I suppressed surfaced. I went through stages of denial, anger, and finally acceptance. I still struggle knowing something like this happened to me. I wonder how many other children, in what was thought a happy home, have the same story.
>
> When my abuse surfaced, I cursed God. But he never moved, never changed in his love for me, not

one bit. Instead, I felt his love more and the beauty of his amazing grace.

When I consider the different depths of unwanted sexual intrusion, from mine to Joy's, there are varying levels of response. For instance, take the example of a wound. A sliver of glass embedded in one's finger will require removal and maybe a Band-aid. A wound from a deep cut may need stitches, or even surgery. Doing nothing to a small wound may cause infection and require antibiotics, while a more severe wound could lead to amputation, or loss of life.

Any kind of wound must be addressed. Similarly, sexual intrusion—of any severity—deserves appropriate attention because it wounds the heart. I lived in denial for fourteen years until a few triggering events disrupted me. I didn't like the discomfort I had to work through, but in the end, I learned I had to move into and through my pain rather than avoid it. Healing from sexual intrusion calls for honest acknowledgement and a process of grief and recovery.

In time, when God called me to write my story, I teetered between fear and faith. Shortly afterward, I went back to school to earn my master's degree in counseling and completed requirements for licensure. I worked at various behavioral health agencies, and then started a private practice.

Through my personal and professional experience, I want to help you recover your hope, restore your sense of safety, be empowered to change, and find deliverance from shame. Although we will draw from various therapies, the most essential source of healing from sexual abuse is not rooted in technique, but in finding your identity in a relationship with Jesus.

Even if you don't call yourself a Christian, or feel cynical about God and religion, hold on, because believe me, I understand the dilemma of the question, why would God allow abuse? The man who abused me called himself a Christian. It goes contrary to our beliefs to have someone in the name of Christianity do what is unchristian. Let me share how I stumbled upon the man who abused me. My story is true, but I have changed names, places, and details.

Background

My body leaned left as our bus groaned around a curve ascending the mountaintop of Jerusalem. After a hiss of brakes, the doors swung open. Fastening my knapsack securely around my hip, I stepped out into a blend of exhaust fumes and hot sun. The call to prayer wailed in the air. My heart beat with wild anticipation as I looked in every direction. Dark skin. Light skin. Beautiful women. Little children playing and laughing in every corner alley of the village. Jewish men with hairy sideburns wearing long black capes. Bearded Muslim men adorned with wrapped headwear. I marveled at people nodding in prayer at the Wailing Wall. Drilling and banging boomed amidst the ring of a siren.

Markets displayed ripe exotic fruits and colorful legumes. Gold, pottery, and nativity scenes filled blankets lining the streets. Pale pink stucco colored the buildings. As I stopped to buy a hat inside Jaffe Gate, I prayed the Lord would speak to me.

Indeed, God had already spoken to me. Just days before we left from JFK Airport, a fellow student had anonymously placed two hundred and two dollars in my mailbox, exactly what I needed to pay for the balance of this three-week trip to the Holy Land.

Twenty some seminary students and a handful of middle-aged couples came along with our group. Our professor had prepped us during our spring semester with a class on the geography of Israel. Now on site he lectured, along with our hired tour guide, as we viewed archaeological digs and historical settings.

On the second day, my professor informed me about an optional trip to travel into Egypt. We could visit some sights, climb Mt. Sinai, and sleep one night at the Red Sea. My spirits sank knowing I didn't have a penny to spare for the added trip, but that felt short lived as my professor mentioned he hoped to solicit funds for a few of us students from two wealthy couples in our group. That night, I prayed fervently God would work through these people. My heart sailed with the hope of climbing Mt. Sinai.

"It's all set," my professor chimed at breakfast the next day. I went right away to thank these dear people for being so kind and generous to a young enthusiastic student, especially to one whom they had never met.

My first interaction with Mike and Nan felt natural and pleasant. With their light grey hair, I guessed they were in their early sixties. An attractive and well-dressed man, Mike's thin frame loomed a head taller than even the tallest guys. His lively voice lifted gaily above the crowd. I learned he owned a lucrative law firm. He had money, influence, prestige, and a polite and mannerly disposition.

Nan, his wife, a pretty, petite woman with a less flamboyant disposition than Mike, engaged us with warmth and friendliness. Though she wore expensive gold jewelry around her neck and hands, I remember her saying one morning that the bagged lunch we were to carry for an all-day bus trip was adequate.

Mike and Nan had an open and approachable manner. We seminary students enjoyed Mike and Nan's youthfulness and humor. They spoke of their trips to their summer home in Italy and their love of the people and culture. In private, Nan even mentioned to us girls that Mike was good in bed. Their presence added a bright addition to our group. Little did we know Mike's interest in women extended beyond his marriage.

Through the weeks abroad my communication with Mike and Nan was amiable. But things changed abruptly my second to last night there. Our group had a special worship night together with scripture reading and singing. One talented pianist, Thomas, asked me if I would sing a couple of verses of a chorus. Afterwards, a few people came up to me and thanked me for my song.

Mike approached me too. At first I was touched by his words. But then he stepped closer, placing his hand on my shoulder, and said my song "ministered" to him.

If I wasn't mistaken, he seemed to be saying, "your song did something to move me and I want to let you know it." Like a tiny flaw in a counterfeit bill, his comment was hardly noticeable, but unquestionably deliberate. If he wanted a response, I wasn't sure what he wanted.

Discovering Jesus, A Safe Man

No one would have ever suspected Mike would use his prominence and power to exploit a young woman like me. I never dreamed that someone who appeared so gracious would make me the object of his sexual pursuit. How could I believe this? What was I to do? Maybe you struggled with the same sense of shock in coming to terms with the idea that a Christian would deeply wound and betray you, someone with influence and respect whom you trusted.

Why would a Christian man use me to satisfy his sexual appetites? But that's what eventually happened, causing me to suffer deep sadness and my heart to rage. My desire for beauty and intimacy turned to self-contempt and self-protective behaviors. How could I eradicate my shame? How would it affect my marriage? Would I abandon the male species? If I couldn't trust a Christian man, whom could I trust?

You may not trust Jesus, or believe God failed you for allowing your abuse. I empathize with you. In my own desperation, I thought of Jesus. He was a man. I wanted to know if I could trust him. In my desperate quest, I turned to every passage in the Bible about the life of Jesus and his interactions with women. I read what he said and did with women and what he did and didn't do. My heart softened by his unwavering commitment to support and validate women, especially women who were mistreated. I can't wait to share with you what I found.

Whether you've experienced a one-time incident, a few random experiences, or on-going sexual abuse, if you carry a past of uninvited and unwanted sexual intrusion and you have not grieved, found the truth, nor believe Jesus is the real source of your worth and beauty, this book is for you. Otherwise, it could help you understand the struggles of a loved one plagued by the aftermath of sexual intrusion and shame.

The Hard Part

Let's be honest. Working through sexual abuse is nothing short of a passage through hell. Dealing with the aftermath of sexual intrusion will greatly disrupt your life. If you choose to face your past, it will likely impact your sex life. No surprise. And you most certainly will experience depression, rage, crying, physical discomfort, painful memories, more crying, deep sadness, guilt, shame, and crazy thinking. And more crying.

What good will it do to conjure up the horrors of your past? Consider the following reservations you may have: You tried dealing with your abuse in the past without success. You're worried about too much introspection. You're frightened about the implications on your partner or family. I get it.

The Good Part

Real change comes in receiving your new identity as a daughter in Christ. We'll discover that Jesus was more than a trustworthy man. He is God. And through his kindness, love, sacrifice, and power, he makes us his daughters. With this new identity you will find healing from your past and freedom from the bondage you're living today. Let my story and the stories of other women be living proof that a relationship with Jesus can give you hope for living more freely again.

Healing benefits may include learning to trust in God, teaching yourself to express what you need or want, and making better decisions. You may find freedom from guilt, self-destructive behaviors and a victim mentality. You may feel enjoyment in relationships, kindle healthy sexual desire and find rest for your soul.

Ask yourself, would these benefits outweigh what you're presently enduring? Does this list motivate you to move ahead? Would you consider the benefits worth the emotional price?

Think about it.

Healing from sexual intrusion is a slow-going, unfolding process. I can testify by God's grace—I am not the same woman as I was long ago. However, I am still vulnerable to the enemy, my flesh, and the world's values around me. I'm still in the battle this side of heaven, but as a beloved daughter of God, I claim my identity in the person of Jesus, by his Spirit. It's good to know I can call upon his powerful name anytime, anywhere, in any situation. He promises to help me. And he will do this for you.

Invitation

No matter how slight or severe your unwanted sexual intrusion, God says he is an ever-present help in times of trouble (Ps. 46:1).

Even if your thoughts about him are skewed and confused, he understands.

Starting a journey is like stepping into uncharted territory. I often felt like Moses taking his first step into the parted Red Sea. Did he wonder if the walls would hold? Let this verse bring you peace and comfort. "This is what the Lord says: 'In the time of my favor I will answer you, and in the day of salvation I will help you' ... to the captives, 'Come out,' and to those in darkness, 'Be free!'" (Is. 49: 8-9).

Where are you in your life story? What might keep you from a healing journey or help you get started?

Where We're Headed

After I share my story, I divide this book into four sections. The first section focuses on why it's hard to tell our stories. I'll define sexual abuse, share a few barriers to healing, and address the need to mourn and grieve your losses.

In the second section, we'll look at the life of Jesus and how he treated women. We'll specifically look at a passage in Mark 5, where Jesus raises a dead girl and gives a new identity to a suffering woman. Jesus offers us a safe place in his family as beloved daughters. I'll explain how to discover this identity for yourself.

In the third section, we'll discuss how Jesus' death and resurrection empower us to change and let go of unwanted behaviors. I've included tools of communication necessary to work through this process. We'll discuss how to manage triggers—the day-to-day experiences that throw you back into victim mode, and how to re-empower yourself with the truth.

Finally, we'll find what it takes to enjoy the freedom to live. When we turn to God's mercy for help, we'll discover the ability to forgive ourselves and our offender. We'll understand how to transform our shame and cultivate a closeness with Jesus. As a result, our hearts will uncover a longing for heaven.

Each chapter is introduced with an excerpt from a poem. In the appendix I've included these poems I wrote during my journey of grief, and a handful of poems from two friends, Amy and Emily, who share parts of their stories. I celebrate the healing in their lives and in mine. As you engage with this poetry, I hope God will use it to draw your heart further along in healing.

Lastly, throughout the chapters, I've included courageous women's stories with their permission. I hope their testimonies will validate your own experience and serve as a reminder you are not alone.

A Prayer

Father, thank you for your presence. You sit enthroned as King forever. I'm grateful you never sleep or slumber. I pray for the one reading these words, for which you have a plan. Reveal yourself to her in a way that is unique and personal. As each woman comes to you, help her see your hand and hear your voice. Bring healing to her heart.

And, Lord, if she is not ready to trust you at this time, please don't give up on her. Help her discover that you are a God of lovingkindness and compassion.

CHAPTER ONE

My Story

As one swift bolt
of lightning strikes
a placid lake,
so his betrayal
left my soul black,
jagged, and gaping.

I was only twenty-three. A graduate student. I had looked forward to getting away for a weekend of fun with friends. I would never have imagined this horror. Still trembling, I was being driven back to my dorm after the weekend was over. My rage erupted.

"You have violated me!" I screamed at the top of my voice.

"Oh, come on!" he burst out, clutching the wheel tighter. "I didn't do *anything to you!*"

"You violated me!" I seethed. "You don't call me your granddaughter and then touch me and talk to me like that! You have been wrong. Very ... wrong." Sliding against the passenger door, grabbing the handle, my knuckles turned white.

I wasn't going to play his game any longer. Clamping my jaw, I pressed my right cheek against the smooth window glass. Relief spread over me like a cold shower on a hot summer's day. I finally had the guts to voice my anger. But I wasn't out of danger yet. As long as I was in the car, I was still his victim.

"I didn't mean any harm." His face pointed at the road ahead.

Where was Nan? She knew. I knew she knew. Why did she leave me with him, again?

I had gone on a weekend trip to see a college homecoming football game with friends, or people I thought were my friends. Now, this woman deserted me and left me alone with the man who had ruined my life.

What if he wasn't taking me home? What if he rapes me on the side of the road? I could see it now, stranded on an unknown road. Left, bruised and broken. No one to call. No one would know. Alone.

Too late. I had voiced my complaint and there was nothing else I could do. Sweat dampened my shirt as I sat in the passenger seat captive, sick with terror.

The day before, Mike arrived at my dorm on schedule. Tall and slim, dressed in a casual shirt and pants, his bright eyes beamed against his tanned weathered face, framed by slick silver hair. As Mike grabbed my suitcase and plunked it in the trunk, I slipped into the passenger seat, the aroma of leather engulfing me.

Mike's face lit up. "I look forward to this weekend. You're going to have the best weekend. Just seeing you is wonderful." He reached out and patted my knee.

His touch, like his gaze, sent a chill up my thigh. I stammered, "I've heard about the homecoming games."

"I just love hearing your little Yankee accent. You know something?" His Southern drawl slowed. "You remind me of a girl I used to be in love with." His hand reached for my knee again.

What? I didn't know I was a fantasy from the past. *Why does he keep touching me?* We weren't even out of the parking lot yet.

Mike's voice turned silky. "Remember how we talked the last night in Israel?" Again, a pat, only higher on my thigh.

I imagined opening the door and leaping.

I remembered. But it had been platonic in the Holy Land. He flirted with me, but I didn't reciprocate. Did he think I *liked* him now? Oh God, how could a sixty-plus-year-old-man be coming on to a twenty-three-year-old?

"What's the matter, don't you like me touching you?"

"I'm not used to people touching my legs like that," I said with a shaky voice.

Mike's voice calmed with the reassurance of a mother. "Well, just consider me like a grandfather. I'm bringing you home for the weekend. Consider Nan and I like grandparents. We can be your home away from home."

First he touches me. Then I remind him of a girlfriend. Now I'm his granddaughter.

Sensing my apprehension, Mike rested his hand on the seat.

I'll trust him if he can keep it there. I guess I owed him and Nan a visit since they paid for my trip to Mount Sinai last summer.

About an hour's drive later, we pulled up to a stucco mansion with a manicured lawn. With my bags in hand, Mike walked through a tidy garage singing, "Nan."

I waited in the garage wondering how Nan would receive me.

Moments later Nan appeared, wearing a skirt and blouse revealing her petite figure. Around her neck, she wore a gold chain. Then, with a slight tilt of her face, her eyes waited for Mike's approval.

"Well, now! Don't *you* look sassy?" Mike leaned his long torso over and planted a kiss on her cheek.

Pleased, Nan glanced at me with cool eyes. "Hello, Lynne. We're so glad you could join us for the game this weekend."

A queasy feeling raced all the way to my toes. I felt as unwelcome as a stranger being greeted by a yapping Chihuahua. "Thank you for having me," I said politely. It was clear Mike wanted me there. And Nan didn't.

I detected dark circles underneath Nan's makeup. They had returned from Italy only the day before. Without a doubt, the timing was bad. My presence inconvenienced Nan.

They showed me to my room and then excused themselves as I unpacked my suitcase. Alone, I checked out my surroundings. The room bore comfortable accommodations with a private bathroom, but the slate floor felt hard and cold. As I closed the door, the hairs bristled on my arms. There was no lock. *Oh dear God, is this so Mike would have easier access to me?*

I scolded myself for having such thoughts, shaking my head to get rid of them.

As Nan got things ready for lunch, I offered to help, but Mike insisted he would show me around their home.

I followed him to the entrance of their massive home. Mike pointed to a stone-carved door frame they imported from Italy. A patterned rug lined the foyer and a dark intricately carved wooden table stood against one wall. On the other wall I spotted a sinister looking knight of armor standing with a shield and javelin. Stepping back, Mike moved next to me, too close for my comfort.

When Nan called us, my legs felt weak as I walked to the table. Before me lay plates of cold shrimp, salad, cheese, and fruit. The spicy cocktail sauce increased my nausea. Making conversation about our trip to Israel seemed forced. In Israel, Nan's demeanor was relaxed and kind, but now her eyes and smile appeared like an act.

I thought of leaving again as Mike droned on about tomorrow's homecoming college football game. Yet, I worried about what my roommates would think an hour away. They knew this was a special getaway and I couldn't tell them I needed to leave because I thought Mike was going to rape me. I didn't tell the girls on the Israel trip Mike had flirted with me.

Nan refilled our glasses with iced tea as I dipped my shrimp in cocktail sauce. I thought I was supposed to trust him because he was my elder and a Christian. Besides, even if I called a roommate, I wouldn't know how to explain my location (pre-cell phone days). I felt cornered and helpless to do anything but play out this charade until Sunday afternoon, when they would take me home.

So, I pretended. Mike pretended. Nan pretended.

Later that afternoon, upon arriving at the homecoming game, we merged with hordes of people walking towards the stadium. Off to one side stood floats of many-colored paper flowers, but the predominant color was orange, the school color. Everyone wore orange. Orange jackets, orange shoes, orange hats—a sea of orange formed a cold pit in my stomach on this warm fall day. Mike and Nan led me, and I trailed them like a prisoner.

We approached the stands, entered an elevator to the second tier, and walked into a special room. They catered everything—barbeque, chips, and drinks lined a long table and a huge window looked onto center field. About a dozen of Mike and Nan's friends arrived and took places in front of the window or sat in cushioned high-top seats, lounging at the bar with its large screen TV.

Nan turned to her friends. "This is a student we met on our trip to Israel last summer."

"How nice of you to come," one well-dressed woman with thin lips said.

"Thank you." A disturbing thought popped in my mind. Did these ladies wonder why Mike and Nan had invited me?

"How was your trip?" another woman asked.

"Oh, it was wonderful. I had always dreamed of going and it really brought the Bible to life. Mike and Nan paid for me and a few other students to go on an extra three-day trip to Mount Sinai. We met a guy named Phil there and he's planning to stop by here later this afternoon." I found a drink and forced myself to make small talk while the men huddled up front sharing their projections about the game.

After a few minutes, my anxiety rose to where my mind and body could no longer connect, like the room was spinning. My lack of concentration, distracted by the fear of what these ladies thought and what might happen, caused me to detach. Drained, I excused myself and slumped in a leather chair. My thoughts turned to Anna, my friend from seminary, whom Mike and Nan befriended on our Israel trip.

She should have been here. They promised both of us a weekend visit to their home. When Mike's invitation came without mention of her, I felt singled out. Why didn't I just call it off? He made me feel special. What a fool I was. As the homecoming game progressed, I wallowed in a memory of our last evening in Israel.

After our final farewell I had headed up the stairs to my room. "Lynne." Someone called. I turned to see Mike standing alone with a glow in his eyes. His words dripped like honey. "Have a good trip and remember…when you come back…we'll get together."

Why did he talk like that? Why didn't I believe it then? I knew I shouldn't have come. These women won't help rescue me. Surely, I must be guilty of seducing him.

Leaving my plate, I ambled over to chat with the guys and in doing so, I felt I had turned my back on the ladies. But in all honesty, I'd felt more accepted by Mike than Nan or these ladies now so it made it easier to talk to the men.

Just then, as the players rushed twenty yards on the second down and the pep band blasted their irritating tune, tears welled up in my eyes blurring my view. A sharp pain pierced my nose.

Moments later, I heard a familiar voice and turned to see Phil wearing an orange school shirt with shorts and sneakers. Phil's hearty laugh filled the room. We exchanged greetings, but would he see how desperate my situation was? How would I talk to him privately? I couldn't go home with him and leave my things at Mike and Nan's. What would be my excuse? I gave Phil a pleading look, but in the midst of all the crowd and noise, he got pulled away talking with the guys.

Cheers roared as the team made a touchdown. With dread I waited out the game. Mike and Nan's guests finally said their goodbyes. While Nan went ahead to the car, Mike, Phil, and I stayed back to gather the last of the leftovers. As Mike and I entered an elevator, Phil stood outside facing me. This time his eyes locked with mine. His eyebrows drew together in concern. As the doors closed, the elevator swooped under my feet. Unseen as a spider's web, I had flown straight into Mike's trap.

Mike and I stood side-by-side alone in a claustrophobic elevator. I anguished feeling Mike staring down at me. I glanced cautiously to see his piercing eyes consume me. In torturous dread, I knew not, what would come.

Returning home, Mike suggested a moped ride on the grounds of their estate. He called to Nan, "Do you want to come with us?"

She shook her head no.

Oh please. I didn't want to be alone with Mike.

Mike got out the moped from the garage and tried to crank it. I clamped my mouth to keep my teeth from chattering as I imagined straddling my legs, holding onto him from behind. He cranked the moped again and again, but it wouldn't start. Mike cussed and threw his hands up, then suggested we go in the van.

Following on autopilot, I got in.

First, he pointed out the window to their acres of property as we drove along. Then, we stopped in front of a foreboding tower and climbed a spiral staircase leading up to an apartment overlooking a manmade lake.

Walking toward the window, I kept talking as sunlight melted under the horizon. Mike pointed to his daughter's house across on the other side. The air felt electric between my body and Mike's. He wore a queer expression I couldn't interpret. He said, "We better go."

Back in the van, we pulled up to a smaller building with Mike's office and Nan's pool. Upon entering, the warm scent of chlorine bid me to relax, but I knew I mustn't.

"Let me show you the fountain lights." Mike went around a corner for a second.

As I stared, mesmerized by the colored lights beaming on the walls, the sound of bubbling water roused me. From behind, Mike pressed his waist against my back, as his hands rubbed my ribcage on each side. His warm face slid beside mine and he kissed my cheek.

"You're so sweet."

Red sirens fired inside me. *So this is the love of a grandfather? Heck, no! If I fight, he'll rape me in this building, where no one can hear me scream.* I stiffened my elbows frozen in fear and a few moments later Mike pulled away.

I turned and faltered in the hallway and tried to collect myself as he turned off the fountain lights. Again, he came close behind me and kissed my cheek three times, "Thanks for being so patient with me, for letting me love you."

What an idiot. How dare he! Removing his hands from my waist, I got in the van trembling. The night had fallen dark and cool. I felt completely powerless.

As we headed toward the house, sweat poured from my armpits. Though Mike hadn't gotten further with his intentions, still…he had tarnished his marriage with me. I sat thunderstruck at Mike's infidelity and now I must face Nan. She would be furious if she knew.

My chest pounded as we entered the porch where dusky shadows hid Nan's face. She quietly sat, rocking. I found a rocker and tried easing myself back and forth. Instantly, Nan said, "You know it's dark and we need to get dinner."

Mike shot back, "I was showing her the office."

I couldn't tell Nan what happened. She'd blame me and what would I do with two angry people?

Nan and Mike went back inside, leaving me alone on the porch in the cold night. I could hear them quarreling, and then fifteen minutes later, they came back out and the three of us headed to a country club for dinner. At the table, Mike's face was sullen. Nan's eyes darted from him to me as if to figure out exactly what did happen. To combat my nervousness, I chattered like a magpie.

After dinner, we visited Mike and Nan's daughter, Michele, who lived across the lake from their house. Michele looked like a cross between her parents—she had Mike's height and her face resembled Nan.

Mike sat far from me across the family room, still looking glum. He crossed his legs and folded one arm under the other and placed his chin in his hand. Michele kindly conversed with me and pointed to a young Italian woman in a family picture on the wall. I wondered if this woman was one of Mike's "friends."

Upon our return home, I went to my room and sat on the edge of the bed, clenching my hands and swinging my legs from side to side to keep them from shaking. *Would Mike come to rape me? How would I defend myself?* Rising, I slid my suitcase in front of the door. Then I sat and waited and just before midnight, I decided to call my roommates. Removing the suitcase and sneaking across the dark hallway, I stopped at Mike and Nan's open door and listened to the slow, rhythmic sound of their breathing.

My heart pulsed in my throat and with trembling hands, I brought the wireless phone from the kitchen back to my room, dialed the school and waited. Hearing a kind voice at the other end, I froze. *Didn't I deserve this? I brought this on myself. How could I explain my location? How absurd calling in the middle of night.* I hung up. Placing my head in my hands, tears fell from my face. *I was in a hopeless situation, and it was all my fault.*

Now, the only thing to do was to go to bed. Since Mike was sleeping soundly, I figured surely he wouldn't come to my room. Fully clothed, I pulled the covers to my chin. The instant my head touched the pillow, a shrill train whistle blasted while the chug of a heavy engine rolled outside my bedroom wall. Yanking straight up in bed, I let out a gasp. Where had that come from?

My body shook uncontrollably, and I thrashed throughout the night. Before sunrise, I changed into my church attire and packed my bag. My eyes felt like I had sticks in them and I yawned when a knock sounded and a gentle voice came through my door. "Lynne, are you awake? Can I get you some coffee?" It was Nan. I beckoned her to come in.

Dressed in a robe, she entered the room and spotted my suitcase. Our eyes met. For the first time, a look of pity softened her expression. But she was too late. The damage had been done. I looked back at her with exasperation. *You aren't protecting me.* She turned and left.

Five minutes later, I bolstered the courage to enter the kitchen. Nan prompted Mike to read a devotion to us at the breakfast table while I ate cereal.

Running late to church, we stood in a dim hallway off the main sanctuary waiting to take our seats. An odor of moldy carpet and the flute-like humming sound of the organ set my nerves on edge. While Nan's small frame stood two feet in front of me, Mike's shoulders towered close behind me. His breath warmed my neck as his hand fingered my hair. *In church and with his wife right here!* I could slap him.

Before the hymn finished, we filed down a pew and to my surprise, a familiar face stood behind the pulpit. Why, he was a fellow I'd met on the Israel trip! I didn't know he was a pastor. *Maybe he will rescue me.*

Then again, since Mike served as a deacon and he owned a profitable company, I couldn't make a scene. My body sank on that hard wooden bench like a stuck piece of chewing gum, and I was further sickened by a sermon about sexual purity.

A forceful wind blew the car and my thoughts back to reality as Mike drove me back to my grad school. At last, the familiar road came in sight yielding my pathway to freedom. As I spotted my dorm nestled in the pine trees, I felt like a hostage anticipating release.

Opening the car door, the pungent smell of autumn leaves turning brown in the sunshine brought me to my senses while Mike got my suitcase out of the trunk.

In parting, my legs buckled on the gravel driveway. I looked up at Mike.

Bending forward, Mike whimpered, "I'm sorry. Really. I really am." The light in his eyes faded. "I didn't mean to hurt you. I'm so, so sorry."

This was the part where I was supposed to say thank you for our time, but not even the good girl in me could say thank you. I wanted to spit. Turning on my foot, I strode with disgust toward my dorm and swung open the door, entered my room, and fell on my pillow.

PART ONE

What Does Healing Look Like?

CHAPTER TWO

Why Is it So Hard to Talk About?

There are times when
I see my reflection,
I hate what
I long to believe.

Fourteen Years After My Weekend with Mike and Nan

Morning sunlight flickered through my bedroom window as I pulled on my purple crepe dress getting ready for church. My hair looked smooth and long, but I felt unhappy. A wave of anxiety surged in my chest.

Slut.

Cold tears stung my eyes.

Stupid!

Misery plagued me whenever I got dressed up. It was my norm. No matter how hard I tried to run from my shame, I couldn't shake my self-loathing. My desire to feel beautiful was dashed to the ground much like riders getting bucked off their broncs at Ed Brown's rodeos.

I wonder if you can relate to my struggle? Whether it's blemishes, bulges, or bad hair, the world's values tug at our hearts and minds. We search for a trendy outfit, try to lose weight, and find the perfect hair color. But why?

Because God designed us to desire beauty. And where there is sexual abuse or sexual intrusion, there is a battle for beauty.

Survivors of sexual intrusion live with symptoms that creep into their lives sometimes years afterward. For example, I experienced these shameful feelings just getting ready for the day.

At first, you may not recognize the struggle as a symptom of sexual abuse, but a further look uncovers how the symptoms connect to our experiences. Before we process sexual abuse, we must identify the hindrances that keep us from healing. Once we label the barriers, we can chisel through the walls we've constructed around ourselves.

I'd like to suggest a few barriers that deter us from dealing with abuse. Perhaps you can identify with them.

Shame

The most common barrier to healing from sexual intrusion is shame. Shame is a terrible feeling that we are not acceptable. Shame causes us to turn against our good desires. Other feelings associated with shame are worthlessness, anger, guilt, sadness, and depression.

A friend of mine, Helena shared:

> What haunted me was how my heart grew numb. I didn't know how to feel anymore. It was my only way to cope. I experienced confusion in my heart about knowing what love was. For decades, I felt voiceless, and I learned a victim mentality. I coped by staying busy and looking competent all the time to help me not feel the shame.

Denial

There are painful memories that women don't want to resurface. One woman expressed her trauma when at fourteen, her family came home from living overseas and her cousin inappropriately touched her while playing hide and seek. Another woman, at the age of nineteen, described her shock when a family friend offered to let her drive his new pick-up truck and groped her while she drove. Women remember the sadness they felt when they lost their virginity to someone they didn't love, or getting pregnant by someone to whom they had never given consent to have sex. Others recount the paralyzing fear they experienced when a family member molested or raped them. These traumatic experiences cause intense anxiety and lead to a reluctance to revisit these troubling memories.

Negative Self-Talk

Negative self-talk is another barrier to healing. For example, after the weekend I visited Mike and Nan, I developed the message, *I'm a slut*. Surely, I was a bad girl. I was an easy girl. I *let* him abuse me. Why didn't I confront his flirtation or stick up for myself? Now my worth was reduced to the muck congealing on the bottom of a garbage can.

One woman, Julie, described her misery. She babysat for the music director at her church. While driving home, he stopped and kissed her and eventually, one day he raped her. She felt partly responsible. For years, she believed her involvement, though passive, was immoral, and that she deserved God's punishment.

Sexual abuse holds the power to make you hate yourself.

Double Think

Double think is holding two contradicting truths or thoughts at the same time in order to survive living in a dysfunctional home or relationship. In Diane Langberg's *On the Threshold of Hope*, she describes the concept:

> One aspect of that task [doublethink] was to find a way to absolve your caretakers so you could continue to feel cared for or safe. For example, on the one hand you may have thought that your mommy and daddy were dangerous and negligent people, while at the same time you thought that they would take good care of you. Another example of doublethink is thinking on the one hand that you have no hope of escape and on the other hand that it will be better tomorrow. (Langberg, 1999, p. 122)

This barrier causes you to face a harsh reality—that what you trusted or had to do to survive now requires you to see the truth of the situation. In other words, you will have to stop double thinking. Likely, you will need to do grief work over the illusion that dissolves.

Pain Management

Another barrier to healing is self-protective behaviors. When any of us experience pain, we come up with behaviors to manage and avoid feeling our pain. Often these behaviors are an unconscious response to help us survive a bad situation. For instance, one woman described how she felt driven to achieve after her abuse. Another became a perfectionist. One described how she developed co-dependent tendencies. Other women claimed they became despondent as they struggled with self-worth, people pleasing, or the need to control.

Self-protective behaviors seep into what I call our style of relating. For instance, I adapted funky ways of relating to men and women. I was anxious and hyper-talkative with grey-headed men. I freaked out when I was alone with a man in a hallway or an elevator. Routinely, I asked men about how their wives were doing to deflect any possible attraction they might have towards me, an assumption based on my experience. I feared women's jealousy, so I acted overly friendly to ensure them I wasn't after their husbands.

By developing an awareness of our self-protective behaviors, we gain insight into why we avoid our pain. This understanding will offer us the opportunity for change.

No One Will Believe Me

Another barrier to healing is the fear no one will believe you, or fear of others' reactions if you tell them the truth. It's not uncommon for family or friends, teachers, or church staff to shut you down.

One woman stated her parents didn't think her offender was *that kind of person*. Another woman was accused of lying and told not to talk about it. One parent suggested the abuse was accidental, or perhaps she imagined it. Other women felt pressure to avoid harming the abuser's reputation. This only creates further problems and delays the process of healing.

Comparison

One type of barrier is believing your experience wasn't as bad as someone else's. We might think our experience pales in comparison to another's and thus is not worthy mentioning.

I worked in a mental health agency in western North Carolina where I had the privilege of coming alongside many survivors of abuse. Just when I thought I'd heard the worst case, I heard another. It led me to this question: "Who gets to decide one case is worse than another?" I concluded each story is unique to that person.

Each response is unique. Each person matters. Having the confidence to identify and define your experience as abuse allows you to process necessary healing and unfolding from fear.

I'm Partially Responsible

One other barrier to healing is believing if you were a participant, you are to blame. For example, you start out with a perfectly good evening and then feel pressured to go beyond your comfort level. A man may have used his physical strength, or emotional control to invade your personal space without your permission and you ended up with a date rape or subsequent pregnancy. One woman explained her anger and bewilderment when she woke up in a daze, realizing she had been drugged and raped.

Others shame themselves for the involuntary bodily responses during abuse. The memory of those feelings of sexual pleasure or arousal brings confusion and shame.

Spiritual Battle

One last barrier to healing is the fear of facing evil. Listen to what Amy said:

> Satan was winning and it made me furious. In the times I felt like giving up during my journey toward wellness, these fears and (this anger) drove me to keep at it. And even though my heart couldn't trust God during much of this journey, I kept engaging Him and remained sure of Biblical truth in spite of my hurt and confusion.

There is a spiritual battle in healing from sexual abuse. Like Amy, each person must enter her own battle. Ephesians 6 tells us we need spiritual armor to confront evil. Satan wants to distort and destroy God's intended design of our sexuality and gender identity.

If you can relate to any of these barriers and find yourself resistant to talk, know that you are not alone. Admitting unwanted sexual intrusion of any kind is difficult.

If you have an experience where you find yourself minimizing an inappropriate touch, verbal remark, or sexual advance, it may qualify as abuse.

After years of heartache, when I read a definition of sexual abuse, it helped me put words to my experience. Having that validation allowed me to take the next step. I gave myself permission to be honest about what had taken place so long ago. Realizing I was a victim of sexual abuse set me free to release what I hid inside. This can happen for you.

Definition of Abuse

How do we define sexual abuse? According to the Child Safety & Protection Network, child sexual abuse is "the involvement of a child in sexual activity with an adult or another child (with a three-year difference, with a difference in responsibility, trust or power between them) which includes verbal, visual and or physical abuse." (CSPN, 2013, p. 5)

Adult abuse or assault is unwanted verbal, visual, or physical contact from someone at work, in marriage, on public transportation, or in any other situation. (CSPN, 2013, p. 6)

Abuse includes disloyalty from someone you thought you could trust and also causes a sense of powerlessness or helplessness with a range of confusing emotions. In addition, abuse often happens in environments where there is isolation, lack of accountability, strict control, and high levels of power. Consider your story. How did these conditions shape your experience? Still, the definition is limited and not all-encompassing. Please don't dismiss your experience if you experienced unwanted sexual advances and if it doesn't fit the definition exactly. (CSPN, 2013 Introduction and Background, p. 5) For this reason, I use the term sexual intrusion because I think it's more inclusive.

The problem after abuse or sexual intrusion is that we can get stuck where it left us. Maybe you feel like a five-year-old trapped in a forty-year-old body. Perhaps you feel mortified and ashamed about an unsolicited remark or incident at work. Acknowledging these experiences takes courage and allowing yourself to do so means you believe it matters. Once you say it did happen, you can make necessary changes in your life. Denying it happened keeps you locked in an illusion.

The goal to healing from sexual abuse is to move forward with a transformed heart, a new mind, and new ways of relating. Working towards this end results in newfound joy and freedom. Admitting what happened is the first step forward to unfolding the grief process. What are some of the losses you have never acknowledged or expressed?

CHAPTER THREE

Why Grieve Over Abuse?

> Terrified
> by the storm
> turning within
> I ignored my fear.

Grieving reminds me of the messy crumbs of a French baguette. They show up everywhere! While living in France, on Sundays my husband Jim would drop me off in front of our local patisserie after church and I'd wait in line to buy our fresh baguette for lunch. My stomach growled as the aroma of fresh baked bread, standing upright in baskets, drifted through the shop. My eyes feasted on fruit-topped desserts, croissants, and pain au chocolats lined in neat rows behind glass counters. A petite French woman with a long nose would greet me in a high nasal voice, "Bonjour, Madame."

"Une baguette, s'il vous plaît," I answered in my best French accent. My coins clinked as I dropped them into her palm in exchange for a fresh, thirty-inch baguette, wrapped in a white piece of paper. After hopping back into the car, one of my kids reached for the crusty end and popped its moist interior into their mouth, dropping crumbs everywhere.

The mark of a great baguette is a crispy outside surrounding a softer inside.

Once home, I grabbed my serrated knife and cut the baguette at an angle on a bread board to catch the countless crumbs. To live in France is to live with crumbs (*des miettes*).

The same goes with grief and sexual abuse. Everywhere you go, there's a painful reminder that you live with the crumbs of your experience. You constantly try to wipe the memories, des miettes, out of your life. But they could show up anywhere, anytime.

Abuse has a way of hardening us like the outside of a baguette. Grieving means removing the hard wall around us while unfolding the softer inside, the real us. Both parts need our attention. Our outside crust of fear, anger, and distrust appears tough. But inside, we long to relax and feel safe and free.

How does one grieve unwanted sexual intrusion? You probably think I would advise you to find a book on grief at your local library, Amazon or Barnes and Noble. But actually, a lesson on grief comes from history. One of the greatest teachings on grief came from Jesus in the countryside by the Sea of Galilee, with his followers sitting around him. It wasn't like a sermon in our churches today, with a three-point outline. He conversed with the people, using stories as examples on how to follow him. Here is an example of one of his teachings called the Beatitudes, otherwise known as the blessings.

Grief and Mourning

Jesus said, "Blessed are those who mourn, for they will be comforted" (Matt. 5:4). Wow, that sounds exactly the opposite of what I want to do. I mean, who enjoys crying?

In this simple statement, we learn emotional healing doesn't happen by cutting off pain or denying what hurt us, but arrives as a result of a deliberate effort to grieve. In doing so, we will be blessed. It's counterintuitive. Yet, tending to our losses brings God's soothing comfort and reassuring calm.

In Biblical times, mourning was a set time to honor the passing of a life. When Aaron and Moses died, the people took thirty days to mourn (Num. 20:29; Deut. 34:8). When Abraham wife died, he "went to mourn for Sarah and to weep over her" (Gen. 23:1).

Grieving means creating intentional time and space to reflect, cry, and express our pain.

When I took time to grieve over the loss I'd suffered from sexual intrusion, I parked about a mile from my house in western North Carolina, where I soaked in a panoramic view of the mountains. The stillness invited me to listen not with my ears, but with my heart. Using a spiral notebook and black Bic pen, I courageously wrote down the feelings and thoughts that surfaced.

I jotted down my memories of Mike. I rehearsed everything from the time he picked me up from my dorm to the time I returned. My heart hurt again as a mixture of regret and disbelief coursed through me. His betrayal produced heartbroken tears, which spilled onto the page, blurring the lines.

My fragile heart turned sick with the thought that Mike had intentionally groomed me. It took time for me to come to realize Jesus *was* there when my heart died. Imagining his presence in that horrid house brought tremendous assurance. Maybe God did have a purpose that reached beyond my present feelings.

Another resting place for me was by a lovely pond at a community college. One day, sitting in my car, a blue jay lighted on a branch. His showy flicker of feathers caught my attention. I connected to his beauty as he chucked and whirred. I longed to sing and express myself with the joy and freedom as God created him to do.

My shame collided with hope. There was no singing because there had been no grieving. Could I be beautiful like that? Could I open my mouth? How could I sing the colors or music in my life? I wasn't certain what I had to offer. God used the singing blue jay to open my sad but hopeful heart and stay committed to the process.

Where is a good place for you to grieve? What memory do you need to grieve?

Culture and Grief

I have a dear friend, Arlene, who works as a funeral director. Her gift is loving people. Yesterday, we met for coffee—actually, we drank spiced elderberry tea—and sat in my running car to keep our bums warm (it was January).

I asked her if she could tell me how different cultures grieve at funerals. Obviously, these are generalizations, but here are her observations of various groups of people: Hispanic cultures tend to weep and wail. Black communities often use hallelujahs and emotional praising. Asians tend to be stoic, while many from the Middle East don't want to hear or talk about death. She continued: "the poor tend to have simple arrangements, but sometimes they surprise me and go big. The rich have a large budget often combing through the details of funeral preparations. Yet, depending on the family, they might go cheap, because that leaves more of an inheritance for the kids." Knowing these cultural differences helps us understand our responses so we can grieve in a healthier way.

Culture molds us. I've seen this firsthand in my counseling. Some clients freely talk about painful events because they saw a family member model talking out problems. Others are so shut down I spend the entire session giving them permission to feel.

I find people who are willing to talk about their discomfort and pain are more often able to let go of their hardness. And when they do, the warm, soft feelings and inner longings of their heart are experienced. Their self-esteem improves and they make progress in relationships.

The more we talk about what's bothering us, the less it controls us. Speaking with our voice breaks the power of silence. This is challenging for people who have been silenced for years. The energy it takes to remain silent about personal or family secrets intensifies, and the longer things are unspoken, the greater the pressure grows to stay quiet. Holding shameful secrets can lead us into hurtful behaviors bent on destruction. Only God's grace and power can unleash our tongues to speak truth so that lies are destroyed and freedom can abound. For each time we talk and express ourselves, we find a new bandwidth of strength.

What encourages or inhibits freedom of expression in your upbringing and cultural background?

The Fog

Life without grieving is like living in a fog. You know how driving in a fog slows you down? It's difficult to see landmarks. It's wearying. The fog of grief clouds our ability to focus on work, do household chores, care for our children, or make good decisions about our health.

This fog seeks to smother us. Grieving sexual abuse resembles grieving the death of someone we love. That's because a part of *you* died with each act of abuse.

I know of a woman whose life resembled living in a fog. After her father and uncle abused her, her mother would order her to be quiet and good. If she wasn't just perfect, her mother would punish her. Because she was targeted and silenced, she felt isolated and disconnected not only from her parents, but from her siblings.

Her loneliness felt like a fog.

Another woman disclosed she couldn't conceive of healing. She never knew happiness as a child. The fog from her abuse barred her from knowing safety and acceptance.

After abuse, some women may give up their dream to marry. Others despair of normal relationships because their patterns in relating consist of unhealthy friendships such as co-dependent relationships.

The effects of abuse are so isolating and asphyxiating to our soul, we define ourselves by the fog, by the abuse. But it doesn't have to be that way. As one who has felt the bumps and pains of the journey, I boldly say, "This fog will clear." All your days will not be cloudy. The offender does not have the final forecast. God does. I know what it's like to be faint-hearted, but I know what it's like to feel the beam of a sunray on my face. Where does the fog cloud your vision? With what lie does the fog seek to darken you? Let's find the truth that will clear away the fog.

A Story: Working Through Denial

Grief requires effort and courage to put words to the abuse. Likewise, it takes energy and determination to resurrect and let go of blocked emotions such as fear and rage. It takes guts and resolution.

Prior to our venture to France, my husband and I headed to beautiful Crieff, Ontario for cross-cultural training. Cool summer nights and fields speckled with goldenrod refreshed our spirits as much as meeting other families preparing to go abroad.

Each evening we had a sharing time. By then, ten to eleven years had passed since my abuse. I was still living in a fog. I couldn't see clearly, until someone else modeled vulnerability by putting to words their own grief.

One of the last nights, our trainer Doug, a highly creative man gave his story. He played a soundtrack that charged the air with a drum roll, then Doug pulled a string and a banner tumbled from the ceiling with all kinds of pictures and memoirs of his life. He shared about his family members as if each was a valuable piece of treasure he held in his heart. Then shifting to a low voice, Doug shared about a time he was abused as a young adult.

I had never heard anyone talk openly about abuse. His story stirred something deep inside me, like molten lava. How could he talk with such confidence after suffering abuse?

The following day I found Doug and thanked him for sharing his story and mentioned my experience with Mike. A few hours later he handed me an article from Walter Wangerin's *Book of Sorrows*. Leaning forward he whispered, "This is dynamite."

The story told about a lonely brown bird and a beautiful evil bird. The evil bird sang a melodic tune, luring the lonely bird to himself.

The evil bird said to the lonely bird, "Come. Put your beak into this hole."

Uncertain, the brown bird obeyed. He felt a softness.

"Further."

He pushed harder.

"Further."

He pushed deeper. There was blood, screaming, scrambling.

"You murderer!" shrieked the evil bird.

The brown bird pulled loose. He blinked, blood-stained and horrified.

Next, the evil bird descended upon the brown bird, plucked out its tongue and maimed its wings. Then, he laid down and died.

Alone, abused, terrified, the little brown bird hopped about, neither able to sing or fly.

I felt confused. Fearful. Angry.

The beautiful evil bird knew exactly how to coax the little bird into his trap. He seduced the naïve bird and stole from him.

That's what Mike did to me. I was the innocent young virgin girl, who naïvely fell into his evil trap. Mike maimed me of my voice and beauty, or at least that's what Satan wanted me to think. I'm here to say that lie is not true. Jesus reaches down in all of his grace and makes a way to give us back our voice and our beauty and dignity. He can use the abuse to transform us into a version of himself that far outshines our former self.

After reading that story, I fell right back into victim mode. I call it the Great Disruption. Painful memories disturbed me to the core and I couldn't repress them any longer. Though the story unhinged me, it forced me to stop refusing to feel. Now I could finally label my experience as abuse. Doing so pushed me through the fog closer to daylight.

Perhaps you've had moments like this, and you don't know where the trigger is coming from or how to piece together your past. It's the fog.

What creates the fog in your world? Have you had a disturbing experience you can't figure out? Try to put it to words. Attempt to drive into your fog. The air will clear if you try.

Grief and Triggers

I saw Doug nine months later, at a conference for missionaries where I was surrounded by charming countryside in eastern France. Somehow, unfortunately, or not so unfortunately, I got seated at a table with all men. Perspiration broke on my brow. *Were any of them attracted to me?* Shame and destructive thoughts beat inside my head. *I'm just a slut.*

Grabbing a tissue, I wept until my tears soaked through. Cradling my head in my arm on the table, I sobbed through the whole teaching. As my breath heaved, none of the men seemed affected by my tears. No one asked me, "Are you okay?" Sadly, their inattentiveness only further alienated me from them.

Finally, communion came and Doug took the podium to lead us. While others made the communion cups ready, a woman with a silver chic haircut joined our table. Like an equal with the men, she conversed and cracked jokes with ease having no hint of fear or shame. My eyes were glued to her, dazed by her confident ability to interact with these guys. How did she do it?

Directed by Doug, she picked up the glass bowl in the center of the table with miniature mints, took one, and passed them around. Doug explained they symbolized the sweet unity and fellowship of the body of Christ.

While I felt depleted and disconnected from the body of Christ at the table, my tongue lingered on the mint's smooth surface. Focusing on Jesus, I tried to regain my composure. The buttery flavor gave me a bit of energy and I hoped one day I could act as confident with men as the chic woman did.

After the concluding prayer, a leader who noticed my blotchy face approached me and asked, "Would you like to talk to my wife?"

Looking at his tender expression I thought, *I don't want to talk to your wife. I don't even know your wife. And why would I tell some strange woman, whom I've never met, such personal information about my abuse?* But to satisfy him, I nodded.

A To C

A minute later, I sat in a side room with the chic-haired lady! I decided I wasn't giving her an inch of information about myself. She appeared so self-assured. I wouldn't, couldn't, show her my weakness.

She questioned me and I answered. I learned she was a psych nurse, so my defensive edge softened as she proved to me by the nature of her questions that she had an understanding of abuse and behavioral health. More specific and pointed questions came until I retold my whole story about Mike. I felt like an unraveled ball of yarn.

"You are not to blame, you are not guilty."

For the first time in ten years, I felt a physical release of pressure as if a two-hundred-pound weight had dropped off my chest. I call that day the Great Relief. I was not to blame.

She explained my past memories of abuse were the letter "A." My fear at the table was "C." The awful feelings and thoughts I felt were real, experientially, but not in reality. My head and body reacted as if I were being abused, but none of the men actually abused me as I sat there. There was no "B."

Then why did I feel so threatened by the men?

Why did I feel so disrupted? How did "C" come? How could I prevent it from coming again? Although I walked away lighter and felt less guilty, it would take another four years before I faced the specific details of my abuse.

Again, I went looking for Doug. "You know that bird story you gave me to read months ago? It *was* dynamite. And today, it went off."

The crow's feet on Doug's eyes creased and with a knowing smile he gently said, "Oh, good!"

Disrupted and relieved, I didn't see anything beautiful yet, but I knew God was up to something. The trigger felt like dynamite that ignites fireworks. Some explode while others just crackle or pop. The latter is what happened inside me when I talked to the chic-haired lady. I needed more grief work, but I believed one day like a beautiful exploding firework display, Jesus' glory would fully light up my darkness.

Often a triggering event will instigate grief work. A middle-aged woman came to me for counseling after she was assaulted in a grocery store. This event brought back the childhood abuse she'd suppressed which included a rape, ending in an abortion. Working through shock and denial is a slow process, but healing starts when you admit *it really did happen*. Before you do, you remain unseen in the fog.

Reflect on your losses. Grieve, as you would for a close friend. And though you may not see clearly through the fog now, if you persevere, unfolding one petal at a time, the sun will come out. I promise.

Have you experienced a trigger? If so, how did you react? Let's take a look at how to move into places that feel dark and fearful.

CHAPTER FOUR

From Darkness Into Light

> I feel a light shining,
> drawing me closer to Itself.
> The terror doesn't take over me
> as much as I had thought.
> Those screams
> and peals of laughter,
> mocking after me
> are no longer gripping,
> they've lost their hold on me.

One lazy afternoon Jim and I headed towards the scenic Blue Ridge Parkway. Rolling open the roof, the fragrant sun-warmed air filled our lungs, lifting our spirits from the dark of winter. On our right, mountains folded to one side like waves of the ocean. Each crevice was dappled with chartreuse green. As we drove through a dimly lit tunnel, a thought came to me, *what if there was no way out of this dark tunnel?* How do survivors of sexual abuse find hope after abuse?

Without light, abuse survivors grope through life as in a dark tunnel. Light in a dark place clarifies our direction. God sent hope to abuse survivors through the person of Jesus, who like a warming lantern guides our way out of darkness.

The darkness of sexual intrusion makes our way unclear and confusing. Sexual abuse can happen over a slow period of grooming or flare in a moment. It might take place publicly or in private. A friend shared an experience which occurred as she was walking between train stations:

> A man was following me, speeding up as I sped up, while muttering sexual and obscene words under his breath about what he wanted to do to me. He didn't stop until I pretended to make a call at which point, he said, "Ooh girl, I didn't mean you no harm."

That moment shocked her and held her in shame and darkness until she allowed the compassion and understanding of the person of Jesus into her experience.

If you're struggling with shame and groping in the dark, what or who has helped you find light?

Down a Dark Hallway of Doors

Let me share with you about how I faced one of my dark moments. Healing didn't come easily for me. One day, I drove to a quiet back road where I could intentionally take time to open myself to my past experiences. I imagined myself ascending a staircase and walking down a dark hallway of doors where each door represented an unwanted experience of sexual attention. Screams shrieked from behind each door. Screams I never cried. I had imagined this hallway many times before, but this time as I imagined the darkness, everything in me wanted to detach from the memories, but I asked God for courage to stay present in the fear and darkness.

Standing in this dark hallway, I imagined cracking a door and letting a memory surface. First, I remembered Mike standing next to me. As he pointed to the knight in armor in the foyer, nausea filled my stomach. A distinct sense of foreboding gripped me. I moved to the memory when Mike came from behind me at the pool, placed his hands around my ribcage and kissed me. I froze like an ice statue. My heart raged, "This is *not* how a grandfather treats his granddaughter!" If I had only screamed and pulled his hands away! *Why didn't I run?*

Still present in this memory, my head throbbed like a ticking bomb. Fear. Rage. Shame. In the midst of this room with these ambivalent feelings, a radiant light caught my attention and flooded the room. God's goodness stood and enveloped me. I had entered the most terrifying place of my soul. As tears trickled down my cheeks, God's glory bathed my face in his light.

I wrote a poem of this imaginary hallway. I read it for months until the message freed me. I believed that Mike's abuse would mark me forever and I'd never have a voice. I worried I would never be normal and converse with a man without sexualizing our interaction. After exposing my secret, these memories eased a bit as the fingers of fear removed their grip. My soul tasted peace in God's goodness, and I felt hopeful he would bring me healing.

Facing the Dark

Retrieving memories of abuse can invoke terror and anxiety. If you have recently had a traumatic experience of sexual intrusion or have never processed your abuse, you may first want to see a counselor to help you debrief and validate your experience.

If you are not currently experiencing symptoms, try finding a safe, comfortable place and allow yourself to recall a dark memory. You don't want to shift into emotional overload so pace yourself. You could try envisioning a picture of God's light into the actual place of your abuse or imagine a symbol that brings you a sense of safety. Make sure you choose a good time when you are not hurried or stressed. Say a prayer before you start like, "Lord, here I am. Please meet me today."

It's hard to face the dark. As you brave your darkest memory you may physically react, so please take time to stop and do self-care. I wish I could find a shortcut to this process, but there isn't one. Facing the darkness of your abuse is like reliving a nightmare.

A friend of mine suffered an unspeakable rape by a stranger and slept with the lights on for weeks afterward. Eventually, she forced herself to lay in the dark. I feel for her. I tend to avoid physical darkness and I think we naturally want to turn on the lights in a dark room. We must turn the lights on in our dark memories.

As you are able, face the darkness of your abuse. Go back and think about what happened just prior to the abuse. What was said or done? What happened immediately after or an hour later? Answering these questions will help you break free from the memories that hold you captive.

It may take dozens of times to walk through a dark memory. You might recall one detail that rattles you like the downpour of a summer thunderstorm. Drop it and pick it up another day. That's okay. Remind yourself of this truth. "…the Lord turns my darkness into light" (2 Sam. 22:29).

God's Presence in Painful Darkness

Just as we avoid darkness, we avoid pain. Pain torments us into thinking there is no hope. I recall the anguish an abuse survivor admitted, "I wish I had never been born." You may feel that despair.

Our darkness can both drive us downward towards death or upward searching for light and life. The pain you feel could cause agonizing and unbearable emotions. To avoid that pain, we may binge watch TV or eat for comfort. We may aim for a clean and organized house, or exercise extensively. We may drink our pain away, take painkillers, or delve into other substance use disorders.

Hiding behind these self-protective ways to avoid pain only delays the healing process. In the tunnel of our grief, we have a choice to stall out with self-help, numb ourselves to the point of self-destruction—or let go of our do-it-yourself attitude, setting our eyes on God. Trusting him will get us to the other side of grief by restoring our hope in the light of his presence.

Light In Darkness

It may sound cold and confusing to us that a good God would allow sexual abuse. It will take the grueling work of opening ourselves to the darkness before we see any good from it. God often does his most exquisite heart work in the darkest hour or season of our lives.

I recently read an article on Belgian lace making that serves as a beautiful example of the effect of light in darkness. The lace maker works in a dark damp room to keep the thread from getting brittle and breaking, except for one ray of light shining on the lace from a window, allowing the artisan to see the lace pattern clearly. ("Brussels lace," 2022)

Our perseverance and faith in God's goodness will eventually give us eyes to see an intricate design made from the threads that make no sense in our life. Imagine what beauty God's light can make in our profound darkness. In hard times, the prophet Isaiah shared these comforting words:

> Arise, shine, for your light has come, and the glory of the Lord rises upon you. See, darkness covers the earth and thick darkness is over the peoples, but the Lord rises upon you and his glory appears over you (Isaiah 60:1-2).

Just as Jesus' coming was like news of a light in the darkness for his suffering people, God can bring light in our darkness.

Ways to Express Fear in Darkness

Overcoming dark territory requires battle. Working through our darkness will look different for each of us. We need to choose real, creative ways to express ourselves. What are some ways to do this?

One way we can express ourselves is through art. My husband and I enjoy browsing art galleries. I feel inspired when I consider why an artist chooses his or her scene or particular medium such as glass, painting, or sculpture. One of my favorite works of art displays a dog on canvas made entirely of multi-colored bottle caps.

To guide you in this creative process, I will suggest a few methods. Pick a mode that works best for you or choose several methods.

Journaling

I wrote poems in my journal as I tackled my grief. If you like writing, saving catchy phrases, or taking notes at church, you probably enjoy journaling. Buy a journal—you can go expensive or cheap. You can use colored pencils and attractive stickers to motivate you.

Make a space that feels comfortable and private. I like my back porch in the mornings, where birds chatter and compete for the birdfeeder. Other times, I go to my front office and turn on the noise machine to buffer distractions. Find a place.

Give yourself time according to your level of comfort. You can start with twenty to thirty minutes and increase it up to an hour.

Use your journal and pen to write down your feelings, thoughts, behaviors, and desires. Experiencing tears and emotional intensity is normal. If you become overly disturbed, say you reach a level of six or seven on a scale of one to ten, then let go of the memory. Bring yourself into a calmer state with one of the tools I list in the appendix. You will learn to gauge your ability to persevere during a painful memory and when to take a break.

Remember, grieving hurts and drains your energy, so don't give up when you feel bad. Stay steady but monitor yourself when you've had enough. You may need to give it a rest for a week, a month, or even a year. God knows when the time is right, and you'll know too.

Timelining

Another idea for grief work is timelining. Take a piece of paper, preferably a large piece from an artist pad, and draw a line across the page. Underneath the horizontal line, write ages such as 1-5, 10-15, 15-20 and so forth. You may want to give more space, maybe a lot more space, to a specific time period in your life.

Next, write a word or two describing an event above the age bracket. Then, try to describe a beginning, middle, and end to the event. Making sense of the chronology is an important part of the process because then you can draw some closure and let go of the experience. Otherwise, the unknown pieces dangle in your brain, and remain a source of torment.

For instance, I put a line above the ages 12-14 that says, "date." It represented a painful night so as I wrote it down, an unsettled sensation came over me and I thought I could use some additional grief work. I remembered I went on a date with a fellow when I was fourteen. He was seventeen. I had bits of the memory, but it wasn't until I pieced them together that I could make sense of what happened that evening. He had invited me to a youth church event. I felt both cool and nervous dating an older guy, but I also looked forward to the music and the message that evening. Yet, when we got to the event, my date directed us to a side-room where we ended up making out. I felt both pleasured and defiled. Years later, as I processed this memory, I broke down and wept over that terrible moment when I felt trapped while worship music thumped in the auditorium next door.

Take each event and recall the who, what, when, where, and how, as I've done. (By the way, this was not an easy task for me. Painful, but freeing.)

Mediums of Art

If you hate journaling or the thought of timelining, use another form of expression. There are other ways to use our pens. Draw a self-portrait, a truth portrait, or snapshots to describe a scene. Remember you don't have to be an artist. I use stick figures. Your main goal is to organize your thoughts and release your feelings.

Look for other suggestions in the appendix for expression such as using nature, music, dance, and sculpting. Find one you like.

And remember, calm yourself when you get overwhelmed.

The Need to Breathe

I have a thick counseling book on anxiety that stands on my shelf. Do you know the number one thing it says to do to treat anxiety? It's simple. Breathe!

I often find in a given day I'm moving from task to task and I don't take time to stop and breathe. When you brave this healing process, you will need to do intentional breathing. This means using your diaphragm and breathing deep enough so that your ribs expand from front to back. You can hold your hands around your ribcage to ensure you're filling your lungs completely.

A basic exercise is taking slow deliberate breaths. Start by breathing in through the nose and breathe all the way to your toes.

Exhale slowly through the mouth. You can also breathe to the count of five, hold for five seconds, and breathe out to the count of five.

Call A Friend

Without the backing of a non-judgmental friend, counselor, or support group, we may not keep going when the process gets challenging. Healthy mourning calls for community.

In my early years of grieving, I met with one of my sweetest friends, Jana, who's in heaven now. (She worked in the mail room at a missionary training center.) When Jana heard of my interest in writing, she invited me for tea at her humble home, where she shared her own writings.

From that day forward we met once a month over chef salads and sipped cups of tea. As I shared the ugly parts of my story, tears welled in her caring eyes. I knew she kept my past close and confidential. Even now, some fifteen years later, I smile. God used her friendship to encourage my heart when I doubted that he would make any good come from my abuse.

Who might you reach out to for confidential support during your grief process?

As you travel through your darkness, the ways you express yourself and your soul-care will reflect your uniqueness.

We don't have to conjure up light for ourselves for God created physical light and spiritual light for us. As you walk side by side with him, another emotion you may find difficult to manage is anger. Healthy anger is necessary for healing and unfolding the past.

CHAPTER FIVE

Why is Healthy Anger Necessary for Healing?

> I'm angry with this woman
> for in her silent way
> he abused my body
> struck, downcast I lay.
>
> I've harbored intense hatred
> against their selfish sin,
> my body scorned the hand
> from shameful deeds of man.

Linda felt intense with anger after she was assaulted by a foreign national on a mission trip. She was groped several times by a shop keeper while her teammates weren't looking. Distressed by this incident, she vented to her tour group. To her shock and disappointment their response added to her injury. One person said, "Are you sure he didn't accidentally brush against you?" Their decision to minimize the incident and accuse her of childish exaggeration added a new layer of pain, one that cut just as deep as the abuse itself. She still struggles with anger when she sees those teammates or hears their names mentioned in conversation.

In effect, her heart battled with friendly fire. Only it wasn't friendly. She felt angry and re-victimized. Often the people whom you want to care about fail you miserably at the moment you need validation and comfort the most.

The Need to Enter Anger

Though Linda felt angry, she didn't know how to express it. Christians don't do anger well. We're told to be nice girls. Why don't we get angry? How do we give ourselves permission to be angry?

Indeed, the Bible tells us to be kind, forgiving, and tenderhearted (Eph. 4:32). We are instructed to be controlled by the Spirit if the Spirit of God lives in us (Rom. 8:9). We are commanded to be filled with the Spirit (Eph. 5:18). Certainly, we want to guard our anger, as it makes us vulnerable to the enemy (Eph. 4:27). In addition, anger does not produce the kind of living God desires (James 1:20). Yet anger is an assumed reality.

Despite these warnings, we need a reality check. Of all the commands against anger, we must consider a distinction between *feeling* angry and *acting* in anger. Humans do get angry. Anger festers and flames when things in life, real or perceived, aren't right or fair. Feeling angry is not always sin. Listen to Amy's story:

> The two primary reasons I pursued counseling were anger and fear, both of which resulted in determination to try to get help. I became alarmed by what was happening in me and was concerned about how low I might sink and what it might do to my family. I was angry after all these years that I was still being harmed by previous traumas.

Amy rightly assumed life would get painful and messy. She knew facing her abuse would cost her time and money and she projected it would put a strain on her health and relationships. She came to realize that facing her anger and fear was worth the risk, otherwise she would continue in a downward spiral.

As an exercise you could keep an anger journal for a week. Write down what made you mad and review it. Can you connect any of your anger to abusive or unwanted sexual intrusion of your past?

The Other Side of Anger: Dignity and Desire

The Bible says we are made in God's image (Genesis 1:26-27). This image bears an imprint on our hearts that doesn't fade or pass with time. Claiming our dignity or image bearing identity allows us the desire to treat others with neighborly love and gives us the desire for others to treat us with respect and common courtesy (Mark 12:31). When we fail to receive this kind of respect, we want to protect our dignity.

We *should* feel offended when someone treats us with disrespect. That's our God image speaking to us. Remember our French baguette? Underneath our anger (the crusty part) is our hurt (the soft part). Anger means we acknowledge there is a wounded person inside of us. It's a sign to speak up for our God-image. This calls for integrity. In other words, we desire what's right and good for ourselves and others. Anger is an indication of an offense against our dignity. We need to put the offense in words with truth and grace. The sooner we acknowledge anger and acknowledge our wounded dignity, the better.

Although we desire acceptance and respect from one another, we can't demand or force people to treat us with dignity. We look to God for our worth and dignity. I like to think of a cupcake to illustrate this. God is the cake or the necessary foundation of our value. We need him first and foremost for our sense of worth. If and when people do treat us with respect, that's the icing. It's enjoyable, but we don't need it. Unless, of course you love icing more than cake. At a birthday party, when we lived in France, kids took the icing off the cupcakes and ate the cake. In America, they ate the icing first and left the cake. Whatever your essential is, the cake or the icing, let God be what you feed on. What you get from others is a bonus.

When people don't give us the respect we desire, it's normal to feel hurt. Yet, it's easy to get ultra-focused on someone's offensive behavior against us. But when we find our contentment in God there's less reason to be angry with people if God is our true focus. When our anger spews, it's likely a sign that we're not getting our worth from him but looking for it from others.

Think about your past or present relationships. With whom do you desire respect? Who has disrespected and wounded you? Consider the cupcake illustration—how can you look to God instead for your ultimate sense of worth?

What is your Style of Anger?

We often respond to anger the way our parents or caretakers modeled their response to anger. If they got outwardly angry, we tend to do the same. If they shut down in silence, we tend to do the same. It's normal to imitate what we see or hear. Anger styles can vary. For instance, hot-tempered people might blow up when they don't get their way, or when someone cuts them off in traffic. Others hide an icy cool anger until they explode. And some (like me) ignore their anger and put on a happy face (it's easier to pretend it doesn't exist).

Giving ourselves permission to feel our anger gives us the ability to talk about what makes us mad in the moment. The Bible says, "Be angry and sin not. Don't let the sun go down on your wrath" (Eph. 4:26). Biblical anger acknowledges wrong. It says, "Be angry." Be. Angry. Give yourself permission to say, "I hate what my stepfather did." Or "I'm angry I couldn't get my mom's attention during the abuse." Or "I'm mad when my uncle, who everyone loves, rapes me."

Consider your style when it comes to anger. What makes you angry about your story? Name your tendency. Do you blast off, quietly rumble, or ignore your anger altogether?

Some of us need to speak up and some of us need to pipe down. We may need a cooling off period to sort out how to communicate without reacting. Starting a phrase with "I felt angry when…" is more effective than screaming, "You are such a …"

What Keeps Us from Anger

Dysfunctional parents or parental figures often seek substances, engage in bad habits, or even use their children to meet their needs. When children or teenagers live in such an unsafe home, they have a pattern of unplugging or suppressing their emotions in order to survive their own pain and discomfort. This results in a lack of awareness to one's anger and hurt.

Listen to what one woman shared. "When I was a child, relatives who lived in our home forced me to masturbate them. While watching TV, they laid a blanket over us both. I knew I had to do the deed or else. They threatened if I ever told my parents, they would do something worse to me. I was so scared, I shut down my feelings and remained voiceless and just did it for years until they moved out."

I don't know about you, but I feel angry hearing this story. Notice the fear she exhibited. This woman existed as a piece of putty in the hands of her abusers. A parent figure who should have been protecting her, violated her. She had to do what was necessary to survive emotionally and physically.

When parents live irresponsibly, the child often bears the emotional burden of parenting the parents or even other children in the household. Taking on this role creates a hyper-awareness of others' needs rather than knowing their own.

A survivor of sexual intrusion frequently must surrender to an authority figure and environment in which she is powerless to control. Adapting to a dysfunctional home results in children growing without a sense of safety or freedom. In this setting, a child can't relax and be a kid. It's why an adult survivor of sexual abuse needs to grieve *what should have made her angry* as a child. Underneath the surface of her anger is the realization that no one cared to protect her.

Victims lack anger because they've lost a sense of self. Growing up in an environment with a rigid, controlling authority figure can produce this inability to sense what they need or want. As a result, they have difficulty making decisions, keeping healthy boundaries in relationships, and using their voices to express themselves—all signs they have been robbed of self-respect. Tragically, survivors who grow up in an abusive home often find partners who treat them the same way. It's not healthy, but what feels normal to them.

What about you? Were there situations in which you were isolated and where someone took advantage of you? Who controlled you or crossed the line with your personal boundaries?

The Anger of Jesus

I visited a new church yesterday and the sermon was on John 2, when Jesus got angry. Yes. Jesus. Some think of him as meek and mild and tend to dismiss things about him they don't like or misunderstand. Jesus' anger roused when he witnessed men making profit off people who came to worship. He desired to keep God's temple a house of prayer, its true purpose. His respect for God emboldened him.

Animals bleated. Birds' wings flapped. Coins chinked. Jesus upturned tables and cracked his hand-made whip, scattering everyone and everything in God's holy place of sanctuary. He displayed a genuine response of godly anger. Jesus honored God by protecting God's house. Acting as confrontational as a lion, Jesus displayed an appropriate way of responding to wrong.

When you feel angry about your abuse, imagine how Jesus would confront one of your abusers.

Healthy Anger Empowers

When you hear the phrase, angry as the roar of a lion, what do you think? Do you imagine a guttural roar? A friend of mine, Emily, broke through her anger as she shared her story with me for the first time. She was raped by her friend's older brother at the age of five. When her friend's mother discovered what happened, she scolded Emily and sent her home. Emily had plenty of reason to be angry. Yet, as a child she didn't have the ability to scream in anger.

For years, Emily felt weighted under a pile of shame and self-blame. As she processed her abuse, she spoke of her anger and bewilderment. Why didn't her friend's mother reprimand her son, or call her mother with an apology? There was no protection, no safeguarding for her welfare.

That day, as a middle-aged adult sharing her story with me, Emily permitted herself to feel the injustice of this situation. She grew in her understanding of dignity, and she developed a new range of emotions, including anger. With self-dignity, Emily acknowledged how defiled and abandoned she felt. Her tears of anger gushed like a storm-driven river breaking down a bridge. And we let them flow. How her soul needed this release!

Take notice how the anger evolved. There was no showy eruption, but more of an inner release. Once we permit ourselves to be angry, we release pent up feelings by crying. That doesn't look like a roar of an angry lion, but of a humble person requesting God's help.

Not all of our responses to abuse are sinful. Healthy anger doesn't mean reacting by screaming, hitting, breaking or throwing things. (Although, we can punch or scream into a pillow, or go into the woods and beat a tree with a good thick stick. I actually did this once.) Give yourself a safe space to respond to your anger with purpose behind closed doors and with a safe friend.

Godly anger means standing up for what is right and true. When we live from healthy anger, we put truth into action. We speak. If we are not used to speaking up for ourselves, this will feel impossible at first. We exercise our voice like a muscle. As we train, we speak with our voice to share our needs and wants in relationships. Using our voice empowers us. How many times I wished I had said something in the moment of my abuse but didn't have the strength. The Scriptures exhort us to speak. "Therefore, each of you must put off falsehood and speak truthfully to his neighbor. In your anger do not sin" (Eph. 4:25-26).

As we recognize our dignity, we will be motivated to speak up in a relationship or situation that angers us.

If you try to approach your abuser, he might not listen or respond in the way you hoped. I remember feeling terribly disappointed after confronting someone who hurt me. God gave me this verse: "…appoint your love and faithfulness to protect him" (Ps. 61:7). God comforted me. (He was my cake, my essential.) This moment of truth helped me to focus on God and let the person's response have less effect on me. I needed to rest my faith in God's love and protection.

You could empower yourself by writing an anger letter. Tell your offender how you feel. Keep the letter in a drawer. When a trigger reminds you of the abuse, get out the letter and read it again. It will serve as a reminder that you previously faced your emotions and help you calm down. When you let it *out* of your mouth, you let it *go* from your heart. The anger will lessen. Turn to God for refuge and he will hold you steady like a rock, even when things feel disrupted (Ps. 18:1-3).

At times, we need boundaries to protect our relationships. We may speak the truth multiple times to someone, and we think it doesn't do any good. Staying in a relationship where there are no consequences for actions not only festers an anger response, it breeds more abuse. With the wise help of a counselor or the Holy Spirit, you can bring a loving consequence to get the attention of an abusive or unresponsive person. At times, it is appropriate to distance yourself from such a relationship, keeping the door open in the event they show true repentance and desire reconciliation.

If you acknowledge your dignity and tap into healthy anger, what might that strengthen you to say or do?

Healthy Tears

Weeping doesn't feel good, but it *does* us good. Please know when we cry, God cares. "Record my lament; list my tears on your scroll—are they not in your record?" (Ps. 56:8). My friend, if God collects our tears, (which are often unseen and unheard by others) it means our tears matter to him.

Tears may take a long time to surface. One woman said she felt numb-angry. "I think it was fifteen years before I cried," she said.

If we let ourselves admit our anger, weeping will likely follow. The God of all comfort will comfort us in our troubles (2 Cor. 1:4-5). He is close to the broken-hearted (Ps. 34:18). Healing will come when we mourn, not necessarily the next day or the next, but it will come. "...Weeping may remain for a night, but rejoicing comes in the morning" (Ps. 30:5b).

How might knowing God counts your tears give you permission to cry?

Healthy Anger Permits Us to Pray

I heard a powerful sermon on anger by an influential Bible scholar, Dr. John Coe. He admitted he struggled with suppressing anger and then erupting. He encouraged Christians to explore the source of their anger and use it as a steppingstone to intentional prayer. When you feel angry, plainly tell God about it. Since he knows our thoughts and words before we say them, we don't have to hide anything. We can bring him the good and the bad (Psalm 139: 2, 4).

Healthy anger draws us toward God. One woman confessed God seemed far away as she contemplated her abuse. Life felt meaningless and purposeless. Shocked and dismayed by the amount of anger she felt towards God, she gave herself permission to feel angry. Was *he* repulsed by her naked soul? I told her I didn't think so. This vulnerability helped her hang on and know God still loved her.

When you feel angry, give yourself permission to be angry. The author of Psalm 69 asked God to call down his enemies; to blind them and break their backs. Now that's anger! He asked God to charge them for their crimes (Ps. 69: 23, 27). We can plead to God as David did. We may have an urge to wish our enemy harm. For instance, we might tell God we feel like smacking our offender or slamming a door, but we don't actually do it. We can ask God to do something to block our enemy. This is healthy anger at work in prayer.

In prayer, your heart may swing from anger to praise. David's heart shifted when he brought his torment to God. He started by saying, "Save me, I'm drowning." By the end, he said, "I will praise God's name in song" (Ps. 69:30a). This demonstrates how emotions change when we acknowledge our feelings. Rather than burying our discontent and disappointment, we turn towards God and speak to him. Often, what follows is peace and praise.

Another powerful passage for expressing anger is found in Psalm 109. The writer asks God not to remain silent, but to deliver him. He reminds God wicked men have harmed him and requests he oppose his enemy and charge him with guilt. (I love this.) He begs God not to forget his enemy's sin and to wipe his memory off the earth. David models honesty. "For I am poor and needy, and my heart is wounded within me" (Ps. 109:22). Once again, the crowning thought results in worship: "With my mouth I will greatly extol the Lord; in the great throng I will praise him. For he stands at the right hand of the needy one, to save his life from those who condemn him" (Ps. 109: 30-31).

In Psalm 39, the author admits that his anguish intensified when he kept silent (Ps. 39:1-3). Don't be silent. Courageously admit your anger and convert it to prayer. God will intervene on your behalf. And who knows, you may end up singing.

Dare I Be Angry?

For many abuse survivors, anger is not a comfortable emotion, especially for people who call themselves Christians. Be human. Call out to God. He cares and listens to our cries.

Now that we have highlighted two emotions, fear and anger, I hope this will help you in telling your story. Healthy anger and a sense of dignity will move you out of the dark tunnel into the light. Remember Jesus felt angry.

If you dare to be angry, you will uncover your wounded heart. If we acknowledge our anger and bring our pain and hurt to God, it sets our heart into a vulnerable position. Instead of the sting of thorns and briars from abuse, you will find comfort and peace like a myrtle tree, which is a symbol of healing and recovery of God's people (Is. 55:13).

One of the hindrances to facing our anger is not taking the time to visit our story. Reflecting on your life is an important part of healing. This is part of the unfolding process. A timeline helps us revisit our history. I'd like to share more of mine. I hope it will empower you to move into your own.

PART TWO

New Identity

CHAPTER SIX

Broken Dreams

> Dirty
> little girl
> sad and torn
> crying inside
> used
> alone
> soiled
> and stained
> can she
> come clean?

As a young girl I loved playing dress-up with my cousin. Climbing rickety wooden stairs to my grandmother's attic, we rummaged through musty stacks of dresses, descending in wobbly heels paired with satin and itchy crinoline feeling beautiful for all of the grownups. I dreamed of swirling in a ballroom, and like Cinderella, I wanted more than a glittering dress. I wanted love.

One late afternoon, my young imagination and innocence came to an end. All my dreams for love and beauty stopped short. Everything got distorted.

Do you remember a time when the magic ended?

At the stroke of midnight, Cinderella's dress and props turned to rags and mice. She had no choice but to return to her abusive stepmother and sisters.

However, against the odds, one glass slipper remained.

Despite her jealous stepmother's evil plan, the prince searched through the night for the owner of the glass shoe and found the woman he loved. God is *our* relentless lover.

God created a way to rewrite our abusive stories with meaning and purpose through a relationship with Jesus. Opening our hearts to Jesus liberates us from abuse and sin. God's love will take what's wrong and make it right.

Better than Cinderella's dream come true, is a life with God, because he is real. The path of healing opens by revisiting your own story and noticing the messages that tagged along with you, the good and the bad. Eventually, we will learn how to find redemption from the bad memories, but first let me share a few good memories as a model from which to start.

My Early Years

Have you reflected on your childhood? Do you remember twirling in a dress? Feeling free of cares?

Maybe your childhood was filled with trauma like a never-ending nightmare. Perhaps your mother or grandmother were abused. Maybe your childhood seemed mostly good but had a few bumps in the road like mine.

I grew up in a stable Christian home. My parents met at a camp called Pinebrook, in the Pocono mountains. They married and had six children—three boys and three girls in that order. I am fourth in line, the oldest and first girl. People used to call us the Brady Bunch.

Dad worked hard providing for our large family. He led in family devotions and ensured we did our chores. At dinner, we'd split our sides laughing around the table. On Christmas mornings, he made cozy crackling fires. Dad laid out six stacks of coins for offering every Sunday. His rich tenor voice touched people's hearts when he sang solos at church. On more than one occasion, he gave a needy man rent money.

Mother, a kind-hearted, soft-voiced woman, loved and served us. Though not a morning person, she prepared our bagged lunches on school mornings while she flipped pancakes. For birthdays, she decorated cakes with gumdrops and tinted coconut. Our clothes were folded with precision. Mother found humor in little things, and she displayed unending patience while I practiced piano scales and repetitive exercises.

I shared a room with my sister, Lori, and we often talked into the night. My bedroom provided me a place of happiness. I felt proud showing my friends the pink floral curtains that my mother made which matched the wallpaper on the ceiling. Yes, my ceiling! I used to trace the clusters of flowers with my eyes to help me fall asleep. Pictures of embroidered Holly Hobby girls hung neatly above our beds and on the adjacent wall, a white-framed picture read, "sugar and spice and everything nice, that's what little girls are made of."

As an adult, I have grown to appreciate the Godly heritage my maternal grandparents left me. While eating at a restaurant, I heard them tell waitresses God loved them. One time, when I visited my grandparents in their assisted living home, as I walked into their room, I heard their low voices and saw their heads bowed praying for each grandchild by name.

Thanksgiving and Christmas were my favorite times of year. My aunts, uncles, cousins and grandparents gathered in my aunt's paneled basement lined with blue wall-to-wall carpet. After stuffing ourselves with turkey and dressing, the cousins gave a concert on the archaic Steinway piano. Following pumpkin pie, we divided into pairs and spent the night at each other's house.

Another high point of my childhood occurred on summer vacation in upstate Vermont. At four in the morning, all eight of us would jam into our station wagon with suitcases, a cooler, and a sailboat tied to the top of our roof. When we passed White River Junction, about half-way there, we rolled down the windows, our hair flying, sniffed the cow-filled air and shouted, "Fresh manure!" We called Vermont God's country. Lake water tingled our bodies, turning our fingers blue. One of the best thrills was sailing with my dad. Lapping handfuls of glacier liquid, with the sail straining, we laughed hoping we wouldn't fall in. We climbed mountains, picked wildflowers, and watched the sun melt as cows munched the evening away. At dark, we played flashlight tag in the fields until we couldn't stand the mosquito bites.

My heart warms thinking of these childhood memories.

What pleasant experiences shaped your childhood?

Visiting the Painful Parts: Sexual Shame

Although we may remember good times from childhood, some may have no remembrance or only vague memories of their childhood, good or bad. There may be seasons, or even just one incident that affected our thinking about our sexuality, leaving us with confusion or shame. I recall as a young child one brief incident that rocked my sense of stability.

"Do you want to join our club?" my friends asked in their dingy basement.

I nodded.

"Well, you have to pull down your pants and turn around in front of us."

Wrinkling my brow, a twinge of uneasiness thumped through my chest. I wanted to join the club. I wanted to belong, but I didn't want to flash myself. But my desire to belong won over wrong.

My face flushed as I turned and exposed myself.

Now their turn.

To my shock, they pushed me away and showed themselves in a corner where I couldn't see them.

Why, they didn't keep their part of the deal! Shame pulsed through my veins like poison.

Tears blurred my way as I ran home to dinner.

Sitting in the middle seat with my family around the table, I searched for words to tell my dad. He'd protect me. But I was bad. *What if I got in trouble for doing this terrible thing?*

I fell silent, hoping nobody would notice how dirty I felt.

For years, I dismissed this basement incident. It only took seconds. Why make such a big deal about it? But it only takes one instance to break trust and rock your world.

Yet after reflection, I recognized all the particulars of abuse were there. Betrayal, powerlessness, and ambivalence. Or for a simpler word, confusion. I got caught between my desire to want to belong and something I didn't want. My spirit felt crushed like a crystal glass shattered on the floor.

I never asked for this.

Like Cinderella I needed a rescue, but it took me years to know I needed one. I didn't know God had a plan. Even a good one.

Identifying my first experience of sexual shame and intrusion brought a deep sadness to my spirit. For the first time, at thirty-eight, I grieved for the little girl in me.

I invite you to reflect on your first experience of sexual intrusion. How did you feel afterward? What did your body feel? What did you think about yourself afterward? What did you do?

You may have an experience you can't yet put to words. But you know it's there. Be patient. You may need to give it some time. Do some self-care. Consider going for a walk and embrace the sunshine on your face. Wrap up in a cozy blanket. Take a soothing shower. Breathe.

Then get back to the message. The message wounds. But it's a BIG LIE. God has a plan way, way, way bigger than this message. Hold that thought.

Do you know there is a new name written for you? You don't know it yet, but Jesus is going to give you a name and you will be the only one who knows what it means (Rev. 2:17). The message Jesus will give you is more powerful than the one Satan, the world, and your flesh gave you. He wants an intimate relationship with us. And he is trustworthy and faithful if we open ourselves to him.

Let me encourage you. Take some time to remember the good things in your childhood. What people or events made it good? In a few words, describe your relationship with positive parental figures.

CHAPTER SEVEN

Grieving Lost Beauty

> beauty is
> a reflection
> of God
> but with it
> are devil's
> schemes

$\mathcal{D}$o you remember those awful middle school years? So completely awkward. I remember in fifth grade, when my friend Sloan came up to my desk with a big grin while I copied the day's math problems from the chalkboard.

"Hey, I like your shirt today," Sloan said, nodding his head. His gaze glanced down my shirt.

I cringed.

He let out a snicker, then left. My heart pierced like a bee sting. I didn't want to be his friend anymore.

Lie Number One: I told myself my body wasn't developed enough. I was ashamed of my body. I believed boys were just peep freaks who got a cheap thrill at my expense. Truth: I am God's treasure. He will never distain me no matter what others do to me.

During this formative time, between childhood and puberty, we develop much of our identity. It's common for dreadful lies to form in our heart which stick like glue years into adulthood. Unless we crack the code to these lies and replace them with truth, we can't expect to free ourselves and have true life-change.

We want to be seen and heard by our family and friends, but the lies leave us feeling deeply disappointed and disconnected. Lies grow after an event, a conversation, or even by a careless remark from someone. Our longing to be valued and beautiful conflicts with these lies. Until we identify the lies we may live with an internal wrestling match unknowingly caught and pinned. Will doubt and fear win or will the truth set us free?

The gateway to healing comes by looking into our own story and identifying experiences and lies that take root in our thinking. To illustrate this, I want to share how you can create your own timeline. It involves reflecting on your story and putting this on paper by recording significant events and relationships, identifying lies and countering truths.

My Timeline

Though my first memory of sexual shame came when I was six, I didn't have a specific thought about how it affected me because I was so young other than that I carried an underlying sense of fear and caution about my body and boys.

We played spin-the-bottle at my first boy-girl party. Kissing at twelve was not my idea of fun. While sitting on the shag rug in my friend's living room, my heart ticked like a time bomb as the narrow end of the bottle stopped in front of me. My knees knocked as a gangly-legged sixth-grade boy followed me into a stuffy coat closet. We kissed, wet and clumsy. *Where were those parents?*

Lie Number Two: In order to fit in with my friends, I had to go along with the crowd. Truth: I can be different from others. Since my acceptance comes from Jesus, I can say no to things I don't feel comfortable doing.

In the seventh grade, my parents sent me to a Christian school and I could feel the difference in the way people treated me. The kids treated me with respect by calling me Lynne, my first name, rather than by my last name Straton or Straight-face.

That fall, I invited my friend David, to a Sadie Hawkins dinner. A day later I panicked. *What if he treated me like the boys on the night of spin the bottle?* Unnerved, I cancelled. Another girl went with him while I stayed at home. Sad and confused, I wondered *what was wrong with me?*

Lie Number Three: Dates and guys were untrustworthy. Truth: My desire to enjoy the opposite sex is from God, and he can give me appropriate vulnerability.

Shameful moments persisted. One day in eighth grade, I forgot to prepare a devotional for class. Standing before my classmates, I fanned my Bible open and read the first verse I saw. "Like a gold ring in a pig's snout, so is a beautiful woman without discretion" (Prv. 11:22).

Blood burned under my face as the other kids snickered, while my teacher rescued me and explained the verse. I wanted the floor to swallow me whole.

Lie Number Four: I believed I was a gross pig, dangling nose ring and all. Truth: My face is not covered with shame (Ps. 34:5).

As my body matured, my shame and fear intensified. Upper classmen warned me to "watch out." Carrying this load, I wondered where it could lead.

I wanted attention, I wanted to be known, but I didn't want attention for the wrong reason. We women want to be noticed, but we want a man to care for the person we are, not solely for our external features that will fade over time.

Lie Number Five: My body and looks translated shame and danger. Truth: God will set me in safety (Ps. 12:5). I need to make boundaries to fit my comfort level. I can rest in God's delight and creation of me (Ps. 139:13-14).

Grieving Sinful Self-Protective Patterns

At this point, I struggled deeply with my sense of worth. I decided the solution to answering my worth problem was to get people to like me. I figured if I could get my friends to like me, then I could like myself. Again, the way of the world plagued me. Beauty seemed so important, but I felt confused and had no sense of connection with my need for God. Rather than looking for my worth in God, I chose people.

With this people pleasing mode in mind, I followed the wrong crowd. Bad choice. For about a year or more, a handful of times I dated, drank, and smoked pot. In my early teens, I went on a couple of dates with a guy three years older than me. We went to a church event where I ended up on the property of a church parking lot in the dark and I felt overpowered in doing things I didn't want to do. In both cases, I left with a miserable false sense of love.

Lie Number Six: Physical pleasure meant true love, and I needed to pursue more of that pleasure to feel loved. Truth: Physical pleasure is designed by God and meant to be enjoyed in a committed marriage.

By the time I was fourteen, I learned people pleasing didn't work. Gossip spread around with the guys and girls that I was soiled. And I had no clue how to fix my reputation.

Salvation

But God pursued me. Three girls from my Christian school invited me to spend the night at their homes. He used each friend in a unique way. My friend Jane, a pastor's daughter, showed me genuine warmth. I wondered why a pastor's daughter would want me as a friend.

Before we went to sleep, Jane reached beside her nightstand for her Bible and asked if she could read us a psalm. Her boldness inspired me. She wanted to please God. As she read, a sweet peace spread over me. I wanted more of this feeling.

Amy, a very committed Christian whose father was also a minister, challenged my faith. In her home she freely conversed about talking and praying to Jesus. At school, she talked openly with friends as if she knew Jesus personally. I thought it odd and captivating.

Katie, whose parents were in Christian ministry, showed me a deeper understanding about having a personal relationship with Jesus. She had her struggles, but the difference between me and her was that she prayed to Jesus for help. In spite of her problems, she had peace. My heart stirred. I wanted this kind of relationship with Jesus.

Dianne, Katie's mom, radiated joy. She was for real. While she dusted the furniture, she sang about Jesus. When Katie's teenage attitude flared, Dianne showed patience. *How could she be so controlled?*

One chilly night, Katie and I drove with her mom to pick up take-out for dinner. While Katie ran into the restaurant, Dianne looked up at the autumn sky glowing with a crescent moon and with gratefulness said, "Isn't God a wonderful Creator?"

How could someone know the Creator of the earth so intimately? It seemed possible from her standpoint. Later that evening, sitting on Katie's canopy bed, I turned to her. "I want this joy, this love you and your mom have."

She explained this love they possessed, this personal intimacy, came from knowing Jesus. She shared how Jesus loved me and I needed to ask Jesus to forgive me for trying to run my life my way. On her bed, with a willing heart, I talked out loud to Jesus and admitted I had tried to find love and acceptance in the wrong ways, through people pleasing and following the crowd. I was tired of it all and I wanted to follow him instead.

Jesus' unconditional love met my need to feel loved and accepted. My desires changed as I read my Bible and talked to Jesus as a friend. Knowing I was loved by God helped me find rest. I didn't need to seek approval from others, especially guys. When I remembered the truth, I made better decisions, but even today when I act in my own flesh, not trusting in God, I get caught in the same cycle of people pleasing.

My relationship with God brought more than the assurance of eternal life. I desired to know Jesus. Soon, I got involved in teaching a children's Sunday school at my church.

Despite the bad times growing up, there were a few good moments when it came to dating. In high school, I dated David, the guy I bombed out with for the Sadie Hawkins dinner. Unusual as it was, we focused on our friendship and limited our physical contact. We prayed and memorized scripture together. Through David, I learned dating relationships could be safe and meaningful.

God showed patience with me as a young believer. I had to let go of my people pleasing habits. (Ugh, I still struggle with this.) I needed to learn that saying no to people didn't mean I was a bad person. But I was still a long way off to understanding how Jesus would heal sexual shame in my heart.

Rejecting Worth and Beauty

In college, I attended a Christian liberal arts school north of New York City, where I anticipated dating and finding a future mate. My freshman year, I got a round of attention from guys after being chosen as Homecoming Queen. After a couple of dates, the attention suddenly stopped.

One evening over dinner, I chatted with a friend, above noisy conversations in the dining hall reeking with cafeteria food. "All of my friends think you're hot," he said.

"Well then, why aren't they asking me out?"

His eyebrows narrowed. "Maybe, they're too afraid you'll tell them no."

So that's it! I snapped inside. *Guys are afraid of me.*

Anger and sadness tumbled together in my chest like rolling dice. But I was more than a pretty face. Wasn't anyone courageous enough to discover me? The real me. The part of me who longed to be known. In anger and loneliness, I disengaged from myself. I hated these weak guys whoever they were, who couldn't get over themselves.

My heart turned from anger to ice. I cringed at compliments. How could I enjoy guys' attention if I loathed myself? I was a tangled mess inside, but God prepared an event that would completely undo me.

A Tragedy

A few months before I graduated, three times during my time with God, I had this impression that something terrible would happen to me. I knew it would feel death-like in nature, but I knew I would survive. The third time this feeling of impending doom came over me, I asked the Lord to let me at least graduate from college. I wanted to get finished in four years and didn't want to do a five-year plan.

Two weeks after I graduated from college, David (my high school sweetheart), called and asked me to get together. Although we had gone our separate ways in college, it felt nice to reconnect with an old friend. Minutes before he came to pick me up from the church where I interned, I asked God if he had plans for us to get back together. A distinct thought came to me. *"I have someone better suited for you."*

We hopped into a red convertible with the top down and enjoyed the spring sunshine and wind whipping gently at our hair. Fifteen minutes later we turned from a side road onto a major highway. As we were driving down a steep hill, another car was coming up the hill from the opposite side. The driver stopped to make a lefthand turn crossing our lane and moved painstakingly slow. We could see it was impossible to avoid a crash, and the only option meant David veering into on-coming traffic. I readied to brace myself. Crashing metal, splintering glass, a flying sensation, and we both catapulted out of the convertible twenty feet or more from the car. My heel hit the guard rail on the side of the highway as my body slammed against the pavement. David landed just above me.

I lay on the hot asphalt screaming. "Father, Father, Father!" Searing pain whipped me as if a Mack truck flattened me to the road going eight-five miles per hour. Seconds later, I realized I was still alive.

This is what God had prepared me for.

Lying stuck to the ground and bleeding, before anyone came to my rescue I cried, "Lord, I want to learn everything you want me to learn."

I titled my head and called to David. He lay with his chest pumping, breathing frantically. Even as I type this thirty-five years later, pain pierces my heart. An ambulance took him to a larger hospital than the one I went to and shortly after his arrival he was pronounced brain-dead. His life ended a week later when Jesus called him into heaven. I never saw his face again.

The car we hit was driven by an elderly man and his wife. Both died the next day.

But God miraculously spared my life.

My emotional injuries long outlasted my physical injuries. I suffered two broken feet and a torn heel. I'm grateful for the doctor who stitched it together. In addition, I suffered two hematomas, cracked ribs, and multiple cuts and bruises. My aunt said I landed on an angel. Indeed. Losing David turned my life upside down.

Over the summer I underwent a slow recovery. My body turned from shades of blue, to black, red, green, and yellow. Moans escaped my body while I slept twelve hours at a time. Intensely out of sorts, I tried to get my bearings from the trauma and depression I suffered over the loss of my beloved friend.

In this, God had a plan.

CHAPTER EIGHT

Someone Better Suited

*Your manly strength
surrounds me
with warmth and safety
I've never known.*

While my body slowly healed, I had plans to attend a conservative grad school in the south for the fall. A few weeks before the semester started, I had an unusual dream. At the altar of a church, a young man with dark hair stood facing me. We were dressed in wedding clothes. I woke sensing the dream had a spiritual nature. I thought about this and kept it to myself.

Upon arriving on campus, I got settled, met new friends, and appreciated the Christian spirit I sensed. When I learned about the conservative no-touch rule for dating relationships, I was surprised. Even holding hands was off limits. No one could touch me, and I felt relieved.

Meeting My Husband

The second day of grad school, the guys' dorm hosted a party for us new students. I had a splitting headache. One of the female resident leaders offered to see if this guy named Jim had any Tylenol. Moments later she brought back two tablets. About ten minutes later, I walked into the next room to get a change of atmosphere and met this handsome dark headed guy who introduced himself as Jim.

"How's your headache?" he asked.

"Better, thanks." His kind approach put me at ease and his words felt caring. I learned Jim was studying to be a pastor. Well, at least I wanted to be a pastor's wife, so we had similar goals. Plus, his hair and height reminded me of my brothers, so I could imagine him fitting into my family.

Just then, I quivered inside as if a bolt of lightning struck me. Was he the dark-haired man in my dream? After finishing our brief conversation, I returned to the room where the girls were chatting and asked, "Hey, is that guy Jim engaged?" (You see, a lot of seminary guys were married, so you had to look for the ring on their hand … but even if they didn't wear one you had to ask because someone might be engaged.)

"No."

"Does he have a girlfriend?"

"No."

"Are you sure?"

"I'm sure."

"I *want* him."

"That's bad!"

I didn't care.

After meeting Jim, I confided in my roommate Gabriela, telling her I thought he was the man in my dream. How strange did that sound? She encouraged me, "I think you should pray and believe, until the Lord shows you otherwise. If it comes true, then you know the Lord is in it."

So I prayed. And waited. Was he the one God meant moments

before my accident when he said, *"I have someone better suited for you?"*

Jim and I dated a couple of times and saw each other regularly on campus. We had a mutual attraction for each other, and I felt at ease and completely myself with him. Though Jim pursued me, I didn't feel intimidated by him. I had an interest in having a more serious relationship, but I was experiencing intense responses to my accident and the loss of David.

Due to my physical injuries, I moved slowly and avoided unnecessary walking around campus. On the emotional side, I had no idea that post-traumatic stress would follow. Grief cropped up unexpectedly in the middle of a lecture. Memories of the crash flooded me and distracted my focus. I involuntarily jumped at loud noises. While walking from class to my dorm, I worried a car would run into me from behind. Intense fear woke me in the middle of the night.

After a few months, Jim and I sat and talked about our relationship. My emotional expressions of grief were overwhelming to him. In fact, negative emotions made Jim feel uncomfortable. He had not come to the place where he was willing to look at his own hurts or show empathy to himself or others. He also sensed that I was not yet at a place to be in a serious relationship so soon after a traumatic accident and loss of a boyfriend. The timing to move forward was premature, so he broke up with me. I felt angry and upset. Jim, too, needed some healing and growth in processing his own family history. We both needed time for personal growth.

An Assignment

Gratefully, Jim, and I each enrolled in a counseling minor in our graduate program. The counseling classes we took had a significant impact on us. We broke into small groups and shared our life stories with each other. It was new, scary, yet helpful to find others who, along with us, were trying to understand how life events had affected them personally. God gave Jim and I time to explore, grow, and heal before we continued together.

Nine months after my accident I attended my first private counseling session. Since I didn't have a car on campus, Jim volunteered to drive me.

My counselor, Cindy gave me an assignment to sit alone once a week and write in a journal about how I felt. I was not used to thinking about what I thought or felt. Yet, my counselor cautioned me, "If you don't walk through your pain, you will lose touch with your friends and family, with God, and yourself."

I knew she was right. The part about losing touch with myself scared me. I thought Christians were supposed to be happy when someone died and went to heaven. I didn't understand there would be grief and loss for the person left behind. It seemed unbearable, but I decided life wasn't worth living if I was going to shut down and withdraw from everyone including myself.

Finding a quiet place outside, I let myself feel and write. At first, I dreaded it. Tears flowed. But as the weeks passed, in a weird way, I looked forward to these times. In those moments, my soul connected to my broken pieces. The tears I tried to avoid brought healing to my soul.

I learned crying didn't kill me.

Ironically, in my willingness to become unglued and broken, God granted healing. I don't know how, but the tears dislodged the shrapnel in my heart. After several months, I cried less. However, the survivor's guilt I experienced took years for me to process.

I discovered that allowing myself to feel sad emotions honored the way God made me. I learned to be real. I tried not to avoid negative feelings and I gave myself permission to cry. Grieving softened my heart and hope dawned inside me that year.

How do you feel about grieving your losses? What do you need to be vulnerable?

Don't Know How to Say No

That summer after my first year of grad school, I went on my trip to Israel where I met Mike and Nan. Upon my return that fall, after the incident, I felt confused. I never imagined a Christian man would flirt with me. When Mike sent me the written invitation to the homecoming game, I couldn't say no. I felt obligated to pay he and Nan a visit—after all, they had paid my way for the special trip to Mount Sinai. Though I felt a red flag in my gut, I felt pressured to go to show my appreciation.

Then, after Mike's abuse, I felt like damaged goods. I wanted to continue my practice of good grieving, but this felt foreign. I felt disconnected to other people because I couldn't tell them. They wouldn't believe me.

During this time of desperation, I went to my counseling professor, Bill Crabb . I felt validated when he confirmed Mike's evil intentions. I told the counselor how I kept telling myself that because Mike didn't rape me, there was no reason I had to make a big deal about it. Facing Mike's intentions made it real. He was after me. I didn't want to accept that reality, for it would require me to face my denial and my rage.

As I got better at giving myself permission to feel, other problems rose. I realized I lived a life without boundaries. I couldn't say no. It was not in my vocabulary. Had I known how to stick up for myself and say no, I could have avoided the whole terrible event. But I did know that even though I went to Mike's house, I didn't *make* him molest me. Yet the real issue was, I didn't want to disappoint people. My happiness depended on others' happiness with me. I lived to please others and in the end, I hurt myself.

A breaking point came when I found myself with three dates in the same week, all with guys named Rick. The telephone rang and my roommate handed me the phone, "It's Rick."

Which one?

Tossing and turning in bed that night, I felt weary to the core. I was tired of giving other peoples' desires a higher priority than my own needs or wants. I hurt myself in doing so. Gradually, I became aware that I needed to believe I had worth and it was important to listen to how my body reacted to situations, to give value to what I felt, and to know what I wanted. I had to learn that what I needed was valid. As I increased my awareness of my own sense of dignity, I could say no to others.

Do you tend to be a yes-girl or a no-girl? Often an abuse survivor has no idea she has the power to say no, because an offender doesn't ask for permission to abuse you. Survivors of child abuse and sex trafficking are examples of people who did not have a chance to say no. They did not have opportunities to make their own decisions or were threatened with severe consequences if they did. Realizing they were powerless in their situations and forgiving themselves helps women regain confidence and establish self-empowerment.

Saying no takes time to learn. A healthy person can say yes *and* no. At times, that means believing your feelings matter by saying yes to yourself and no to others. Learning to make decisions based on a sense of self-worth enables a survivor to say no to unsafe people and places. Meeting trustworthy friends, keeping safe relationships, and making a safe environment are necessary for recovery.

Dating Again

That year went by, and I saw Jim in social gatherings, but we still didn't date. In the spring he seemed friendly. We both had done a lot of work on ourselves and by the summer, Jim came to visit me where I did an internship in New York City. Our time together sparked a new beginning. In the fall semester, we enjoyed being together on campus, water skiing, and visiting art museums. The following spring, we were engaged on St. Patrick's Day. I'll never forget the sun breaking through a foggy morning sky on the beach at Sullivan's Island, Charleston when he proposed to me. We married four months later July 1, 1989, three and a half years after we met.

In spite of my abuse, I looked forward with anticipation to marriage and my wedding night. I had a positive view of sex as my parents modeled a close and affectionate relationship. I remember as a kid, feeling happy and secure when they hugged and kissed. They spoke fondly about their dating experience. Jim and I had a healthy attraction for one another, and I had not dwelled on the abuse up to that point.

Triggers After Marriage

Yet, God stretched my faith. I thought my struggle with worth and beauty would end once I married. Sly as a snake, my abuse would rise and rattle its tail. Disturbing triggers upset me while Jim worked as an assistant pastor and I birthed three babes, two girls and a boy.

In our early years of marriage, there were times when I involuntarily saw Mike's face appear during intimate moments with my husband. That sent shock waves through me and I felt plagued with guilt. I didn't understand why this was happening. I brought my troubled situation to my counselor, who encouraged me to focus on being in the moment, in the here and now. That seemed to help. In spite of these occasions, I would say for the most part, imperfect as any marriage is, we felt good about our sex life.

But other triggers came. One day after a church potluck, with others milling around while cleaning the kitchen, a gray headed man helping tidy up stopped and greeted me. He faced me and placed both arms over my shoulders with his body square in front, only six to eight inches away.

My body fired up. Fear. *Run!*

I tried standing completely at ease. But I felt upset and angry afterward.

There is a connection between our triggers and the specific details of our abuse. For instance, when I saw gray haired men or men in authority, I got triggered. I mistakenly thought I was attracted to them. Why did I experience this? For years, I thought something was terribly wrong with me. As I've aged this happens rarely, unless I see someone who looks very similar to Mike.

I also feared married women would potentially be mad at me. I eventually identified where the fear originated—that is when I felt I had gotten between Mike and Nan. Once I saw the connection, I was able to tell myself no one had a reason to be mad at me and I tried to relax. Simple things, like sitting near a man in church, at the beach, or on public transportation, made me nervous and fidget. I had to remind myself these men were innocent. They were just taking up space next to me. But each time, it felt like a battle to calm down.

Does Grieving Abuse Last A Life-Time?

Once I started working on my abuse, I did notice that I seemed reluctant at times to have sex with Jim. We talked about it so I could calm down and let go of control. Being spontaneous usually felt easier than planned sex.

Still, I showed startle responses when Jim came up behind me. For instance, when I worked on my computer and needed help, if he put both arms around me to reach for the keyboard, I felt trapped. It reminded me of Mike coming up to me from behind. If we were out shopping and got separated in public and then Jim came up without saying my name, I would jump. So, I asked him to make sure he would make his presence known by saying my name first.

Other grievances arose when men complimented me. Fainthearted, I froze in fear, not knowing how to respond. I had to sort out in my mind whether it seemed to go beyond proper boundaries. Certainly, some men weren't meaning any harm in what they said and did. I had to be discerning. I remember one man at church would give me a hug and kiss on the cheek, but the way he formed his lips would remind me of the way Mike kissed me. And though it made me feel uncomfortable initially, to bring that to his attention would have made things more uncomfortable. Fortunately, in time, I could relax when I focused on the fact that this gentleman was only being brotherly.

I had a low tolerance for movies, television or news that implied or reported abuse. At times, I would spring from the couch and close the doors to our entertainment center. In fear, I felt it was necessary to block out anything that reminded me of the powerlessness of a victim.

When I went to male doctors, my body tensed in the chair and I'd tap my feet on the floor. I especially had trouble with visits to an ophthalmologist. Sitting in the dark with my chin on a machine while the doctor's face bent into mine was unnerving. On one occasion this specific doctor put his hand on my knee. Again, even though I felt startled and angry, I didn't want him to get mad at me. I didn't feel the freedom yet to tell him he did something wrong. But years later, after I had worked on boundaries and using my voice, a different eye doctor touched my knee and I called him on it right away. I felt empowered by my progress.

The effects of sexual abuse linger for a long time. It's like an unseen emotional scar lying on the inside of our soul. It stings when certain events touch it, like a sensitive physical scar.

As a counselor, I frequently read books and hear stories about abuse. At times, I've experienced arousal when I'm reminded of people mis-using others sexually and abusing their power. These are lingering effects of my experience with Mike. I struggle with feelings of shame and despair when this happens until I remind myself of God's love. His love is greater than my shame. His punishment of sin covers and cancels any harm against me and his peace clears my heart from these disturbing experiences. Like a reset button. It makes me long for heaven when one day I will look and see Jesus coming towards me with open arms and kindness in his eyes.

There are no promises that we will wipe every effect of sexual intrusion from our lives while on this earth, but we have the promise of knowing once we get to heaven, all the effects of abuse will be gone forever.

Perseverance in Grief

As you work on your timeline, think about what happened in your abuse. What was the response of those you told? This will help you understand why and how you get triggered. Write down the thoughts about yourself for each event. Combing through your past can be disruptive. What lies did you believe? What vows did you make? What did you do to avoid your pain? What did you long for in each of those scenarios?

Unfolding - *Recovering Your Identity After Sexual Intrusion*

At this juncture you may feel a bit overwhelmed. Remember our inner beauty unfolds slowly, one petal at a time. Just as a rose begins as a bud, eventually with water and sun and the right atmosphere, it unfolds in its glory. Let's continue to validate what you're going through. You may think your past might make you doubt you'll ever trust again.

CHAPTER NINE

Holding Onto Desire

*Why do I fear men?
Cringing, looking away,
half-hearted conversation,
fear of fear itself—
all-consuming fire.*

Standing before the class, I wrote participants' answers on the white board while co-teaching with my husband at the training center for missionaries. The question: What do women want in their relationships with their spouses? Love, security, provision, protection, and non-sexual touch. These are God-given desires that reflect our design.

We created another wish list for the men. Respect, sex (maybe that comes first), success, nurture, and companionship. After God made Adam and the animals, there was one thing lacking. A woman! When Adam saw Eve, he shouted, "You are bone of my bone and flesh of my flesh" (Gen. 2:23). God's final touch of creation was another human who connected with Adam.

God made woman, man's co-equal partner. We fit together side by side, not only in what we do, but who we are. When a man and woman join physically, they become one. Not only in physical intimacy, but in the ability to join soul to soul. Though men and women may value different things, they complement one another.

But our desires for intimacy often end in disappointment. When we don't live by God's plan, our souls tear apart. Selfishness abounds. Disappointment breeds mistrust. In what ways do you feel that each day?

The Curse

The curse corrupts everything, plaguing us with problems.

Satan tempted Eve to disbelieve the goodness of God.

When Eve, and subsequently Adam, turned from God's way, they were forced to leave their home in the garden (Gen 3). What an unhappy day.

God placed a curse on each of them and in turn, the curse passed down to us (Rom. 5:12). What does the curse look like? Let's start with women. Part A is female pain. Lots of pain. Menses. Childbirth. Hormones. Menopause. Part B of the curse is the desire for our husband. Hmm. Our husband will rule over us (Gen. 3:16). There are lots of interpretations of this (study it for yourself), but in the big picture, a woman longs to be fully loved by a man but, sadly, she feels the love he gives her will never be enough. So often men rule over women in selfish ways rather than loving them.

An unmarried woman desires a husband to love and cherish her. And a married woman realizes her husband's love (as good as it is), will be imperfect. We will never have it all in a man!

A ginormous disappointment, isn't it?

The curse is like a choking weed.

And the curse affects both men and women, so that trusting is difficult. Because women want to be loved and men are imperfect in loving them, trust becomes a problem. Whether we are single, married, widowed, or divorced, we struggle with unmet desires to be loved. I should add that a man desires respect and a woman will never perfectly meet his criteria either, no matter how hard she tries.

Our needs and desires come from God. Yet our insecurities can make us doubt God's love. Thus, we are tempted to shift our trust away from God and focus on men to fill our desires. Are you ever tempted to put too much emphasis on trusting a man or someone else?

Mere Men

Sex.

Such a hot topic.

As I continued writing this chapter, I prayed. And waited a day. This morning, I saw it again. More news about men assaulting women. Satan loves to destroy God's design for oneness between a man and a woman. He delights when women are overpowered by men.

New York Governor Andrew Cuomo makes little of multiple women accusing him of inappropriate behavior. Since I wrote this he has now been removed from office.

A former actress, Rose McGowan, now an activist for women's rights, speaks out about men who "feed off their power." McGowan was raped by Hollywood producer Harvey Weinstein, now serving a twenty-three-year prison sentence for conviction of rape, sexual assault, and harassment from dozens of women.

After Weinstein's fallout in 2018, many high-profile men in entertainment, news media and politics were forced to resign, retire, or were fired after accusations of sexual misconduct, ranging from indecent comments to rape. They include actor Bill Cosby, financier Jeffrey Epstein (who was found dead in his prison cell), Penn State coach Jerry Sandusky and various gymnastics coaches including John Geddert.

Even Catholic priests and leading Christian men have sadly fallen.

I'm surprised by the conflicting responses of women. Some remain silent for political advantage or other reasons. Others speak out like the Sexual Harassment Working Group or those who are part of the #MeToo Movement.

Our trust is shaken when decent people are wrongly accused of abuse. For example, consider US Supreme Court Justice Brett Kavanaugh. Having no prior accusation on his record, Christine Blasey Ford accused Kavanaugh for alleged sexual misconduct (an incident she said occurred thirty years prior). Harshly questioned and investigated numerous times, he was acquitted and confirmed to the Supreme Court.

Bad men.

Good men.

Who can you trust?

Betrayal and Broken Trust

Trust. We seem to possess so little, yet it's the foundation of relationships. Betrayal breaks close bonds. One person said of a betrayed friend, "she's broken because she believed." (Quotessign, 2022) And another said, "I'm not crying because of you…I'm crying because my delusion of who you were was shattered by the truth of who you are." (Quotessign, 2022)

How has abuse affected your level of trust? In what areas would you like to grow in your relating style with men?

Abuse and God

What about our attitude towards God? How can we feel close to God when he's allowed abuse? Listen to one woman who wrestled with her heart:

> I was furious with my abusers, angry with myself, and deeply disappointed with God. The rage I felt was so intense I wanted to shatter a chair with a baseball bat! This desire to destroy was alarming. I realized I'd been punishing myself and could probably shred someone.

Even though a woman ends up a victim of abuse and unspeakable suffering, shutting down and closing God out is sin. Without reliance on God's love and forgiveness, our sin leaves us enslaved to ourselves.

Listen to one woman's thoughts about God the Father. (She witnessed a man exposing himself on a train.) During a time of ministry, she said:

> "I remember one time out on a prayer walk, I made a derogatory remark against the 'Johns' who were picking up prostitutes in front of us. The woman I was walking with said, "These men are someone's husband, brother, son, uncle ..." It humanized them ... they weren't just monsters anymore.
>
> It breaks my heart to think about men and women, boys and girls who have suffered sexual abuse. What encourages me and comforts me is knowing that God's own heart was broken.
>
> He sent fire down from heaven to destroy Sodom and does not turn away from what is happening all over the earth. The wickedness will be exposed and answered for ... if not at the Cross, then in the lake of fire (Rev. 20).
>
> I'm so thankful that my Heavenly Father doesn't leave these terrible things undealt with. It would be unbearable otherwise."

It was wrong that someone invaded your space and your body and your mind. Your offender will be judged by God. Rest in knowing that. On the same note, have you come to a place where you realize you also are a sinner needing God's forgiveness?

Can We Trust God to Judge Wicked Men?

Psalm 10 reveals God's heart towards people who are evil. It starts out with a question probably like one you or I have posed sometime in our lives. "Lord, why do you hide yourself in times of trouble?"

Doesn't that sound like a question we have asked?

Wicked men hunt down people who are weak and they devise evil schemes. A wicked man crushes his victims. He is proud and prosperous and doesn't suspect God will destroy him. But the writer shouts to God, "Arise!" It's like he's saying, don't forget us, the helpless little people who don't have a voice, or a good lawyer.

God does see our trouble and grief. Truly, the Lord will hear those in pain. The Bible clearly says of our God, "You hear the desire of the afflicted; you encourage them, and you listen to their cry, defending the fatherless and the oppressed, in order that man, who is of the earth, may terrify no more" (Ps. 10:18). The Word encourages victims to commit themselves to the Lord. He'll break down and destroy those who do wrong and call them to account for themselves. He may not accomplish that today, but a judgment day is near. "But for the cowardly and unbelieving and abominable and murderers and immoral persons and sorcerers and idolaters and all liars, their part will be in the lake that burns with fire and brimstone, which is the second death" (Rev. 21:8 NASB).

How does the passage above move you? Knowing God will ultimately do away with evil doers and defend our cause can assure us that he hears us and will punish our abusers. Cry out to him even if, at the moment, you don't understand everything. He is trustworthy.

Good Men

God has blessed me and used some godly men as powerful agents to bring healing in my life. But I've also learned to shift the focus of my heart from men to God. Men will fail me. And I fail too, in my relationships with them.

In short, all women, especially those who've survived sexual abuse and assault, must consider the trustworthiness of each man with whom they are in relationship. Our level of trust depends largely on what kind of men we choose to enter our lives. Gratefully, even when women have experienced sexual intrusion, God does use safe, trustworthy men to bring healing whether they be father figures, brothers, husbands, friends, spiritual leaders or counselors.

I have personally benefited from the trust I've developed with men in my life. I'm grateful for the safety I sensed from Pete, my counselor. I've enjoyed relationships with men in my small group at church. And then there is my husband, Jim, who has loved me in spite of all the ways my sexual intrusion has affected me.

What men have offered good gifts to you?

Holding On to Desire When Trust Is Broken

We thirst for love and intimacy. It's the way God made us. But sin has caused a dilemma. The curse has made our unmet desires painful. You may have heartbreaking disappointments in relationships with destructive men. Even the best of men, who love Jesus, will disappoint us. Jesus is the one man that will never fail us.

What difference would if make if you opened the desires of your heart and put your trust in him? Imagine your heart unfolding from a bud to a rose. Let's take a look at how Jesus treated women. Is Jesus a trustworthy man?

CHAPTER TEN

Is Jesus a Trustworthy Man?

>Resting
>in His joy
>resting
>in His smile
>
>I love to feel
>His peace
>and rest
>in Him awhile.

---

*O*ne day just as I noticed my spring bulbs poking their green tops through the black soil, I believe God gave me an idea. I thought if Jesus is trustworthy, I needed to know how he related to women. Also, how did Jesus treat children? I felt the answer to those questions would tell me whether he was trustworthy. I combed through every Bible passage in the Gospels of Matthew, Mark, Luke, and John (books written about the life of Jesus) having to do with Jesus and his interactions with women and children and was amazed by what I found. I would encourage you to find a Bible with an easy-to-read translation and look for yourself.

Could Women and Children Trust Jesus?

Starting with Matthew, here's what I discovered. Never did Jesus look at, talk to, or touch a woman inappropriately. In many cases, he was not the initiator between a woman and himself. Think on that for a good minute. If Jesus had no ill reputation, why wouldn't he be trustworthy?

Jesus let women approach him. The sinful woman wept at his feet (Matt. 26). The suffering woman touched his garments (Mk. 5). According to scripture, he never touched the woman caught in adultery (Jn. 8). Mary Magdalene clung to him after his resurrection, but Jesus never had a relationship other than friendship with her (Jn. 20:17).

In a couple of cases, Scripture tells us Jesus took someone by the hand. When Jesus healed Peter's mother-in-law, he took her by the hand and her fever left (Matt. 8). He took Jairus' daughter's hand and lifted her from her death bed (Mk. 5). Jesus was trustworthy with his touch.

Children could trust Jesus because he didn't touch children inappropriately. For example, when the disciples discouraged children to come to Jesus, he rebuked them. Instead, he lovingly gathered the children in his arms, and blessed them (Mk. 10:13-16). These moments with children were in public settings.

Jesus strongly opposed anyone who caused harm to a child. In fact, he declared that anyone who made a child sin or suffer deserved death (drowned in the sea, Mk. 9:42). Jesus defended the innocence and safety of anyone vulnerable in his day, which certainly included women and children.

Once, Jesus brought a small child beside him as his disciples argued who would be the greatest. He said, "Whoever welcomes this little child in my name welcomes me; and whoever welcomes me welcomes the one who sent me. For he who is least among you all—he is the greatest" (Lk. 9:48). Jesus taught that having the humility or gentleness of a child would make someone great.

As a survivor of child sexual abuse, what might these truths mean to you? How would Jesus feel about your childhood abuse?

The Kindness and Gentleness of Jesus

At the age of thirty, Jesus began preaching and performing miracles for people to see God's love through his life. Jesus healed people from all kinds of sicknesses. During this time, many women followed him and helped take care of his physical needs. Among the women were Mary Magdalene, the mother of Zebedee's sons, Mary (the mother of James and Joses), Salome, Joanna and Susanna (Lk. 8:1-3).

Though Jesus was never guilty of ill treatment towards a woman or child, he was crucified for claiming he was the Son of God (Lk. 22:69-71). Even when Pilate found no basis for charges against Jesus, he gave the order to have him beaten (Lk. 23:14-25). As Jesus hung on the cross, he cried out, "Father, forgive them for they do not know what they are doing" (Lk. 23:34). A sign, 'King of the Jews' was posted on the cross from which he hung. In his last moments, he mercifully spared a criminal a life of torment in hell.

Many people mourned Jesus' death. As he was dying, Jesus asked John to take care of his mother (Jn. 19:26). He cared for the welfare of women who needed provision by calling out to those standing close by, "Daughters of Jerusalem, do not weep for me; weep for yourselves and your children" (Lk. 23:28).

As Jesus gave up his last breath, the sky turned black and the veil in the temple tore in two, separating the spiritual barrier between God and man. A centurion praised God and said, "Surely this was a righteous man." Others beat their breasts and walked away, but the women Jesus knew and loved stood from a distance watching (Lk. 23:27-49).

How does your heart respond to Jesus' kindness toward women?

Jesus' Miracles in Ministry

According to Scripture, Jesus was more than a man. He was sent from God, and he was God (Jn. 1:1). He was the Son of God and bore the perfect image of God (Col.1:15-20). He performed miracles to reveal God's love and power to people (Jn. 10:38).

Jesus' first miracle occurred at a wedding where the host ran out of wine (Jn. 2:1-11). This would be like running out of food. Mary, Jesus' mother, asked him to help the host. Though it wasn't time for Jesus to shed his blood, he honored his mother's request by changing six huge vats of water into fine wine, saving the host from social disgrace. (Tenney, 1981) This miracle suggested Jesus' life-giving blood, like fine tasting wine, saves us from our sins. (Tenney, 1981) Those who believe in the sacrifice he made on our behalf, the shedding of his blood, will one day join the wedding feast in heaven (Rev. 19:7-10).

In several healings, Jesus risked social and spiritual judgment to meet the need of a woman. This is one of my personal favorites. While walking through the town of Nain, a funeral procession slowed his passage. A widow, whose only son had died, followed alongside the casket. Moved with compassion by her tears, Jesus said, "Don't cry." Touching the coffin (making himself ceremonially unclean under Hebrew law), he raised up her son and gave him back to his mother (Lk. 7:11-17).

Jesus comforted grieving women. Sisters Mary and Martha watched with grief-stricken hearts as their brother Lazarus got sick and died. It pained them to bury him without Jesus present. But when Jesus arrived, he wept with them. He said, "I am the resurrection and the life" (Jn. 11:25). Jesus raised their brother Lazarus from the dead. Many people believed upon witnessing

Jesus' authority and power. But the Pharisees and the religious plotted to kill him (Jn. 11:17-57).

Women's physical ailments and chronic illnesses were restored. Placing his hands on a woman who was crippled for eighteen years, Jesus freed her from an evil spirit (Lk. 13:10-17). He freed another woman who had continuous bleeding for twelve years (Mk. 5:25-34).

What would it mean to you if Jesus risked social embarrassment to help you? If you believe Jesus cared about these women's needs, how might this help you trust he will care for you?

Jesus' Attitude Towards Women

Jesus accepted women as his mothers, sisters and daughters. He said, "For whoever does the will of my Father in heaven is my brother and sister and mother" (Matt. 12:50). How might this lead you to do God's will?

When women gave sacrificially, Jesus noticed. For example, he saw a poor widow giving a few coins for an offering compared to the rich people who gave from their abundance (Luke 21:1-4). Though no one else may know, you can have confidence Jesus sees your love and deeds done by faith large or small.

Jesus recognized the faith of women especially those who lived on the fringes of society. A Canaanite woman (a non-Jewish person) asked Jesus to heal her demonized daughter. At first, Jesus ignored her request, because his ministry to the Jews was his first calling (Rom. 11:11; Later the Gentiles, or non-Jews, were brought into his family). Yet, this woman appealed to him. "Lord, help me!" she said. When Jesus still hesitated, she appealed to his kindness. In effect she said: Even a fringe person like me (a dog or a nobody) eats savory table scraps from his masters' table. Astounded by her faith, Jesus approved her request and healed her daughter (Matt.15: 21-28).

How might this help you ask Jesus for something you don't think you deserve?

This story makes me think of people in our world who are hated or misunderstood. I'm thinking of people who may be viewed as culturally inferior, or who may have a disadvantage compared to others. Whether it's a matter of education, status, money, possessions, politics, or gender, if you are feeling like a loner, remember that Jesus, God's kind Son, will receive you regardless of your past, your exterior, or whatever else might cause others to dismiss you. How could believing in Jesus' kindness increase your faith in him?

A Socially Outcast Woman

Speaking of loners or outsiders, let's consider how Jesus interacted with three sinful women.

Tired and thirsty from travel, Jesus and his disciples stopped to get lunch in a town populated with outcasts and minorities. While the disciples searched for food, Jesus sat at a famous well. Think of Times Square.

A sinful woman drew water mid-day to avoid the snarky gossip of other women. (Ever felt rejected by other women?) In that culture, men didn't speak to women, nor did Jews speak to half-Jews, so Jesus' question disarmed her.

"Could you give me a drink?"

"Why are you talking to me?" *I'm the hated minority and outcast here.*

"If you knew who I am, you'd be asking me for a drink," Jesus said.

"Are you better than Jacob who gave us this well?"

Jesus draws her back to her thirst. "My water will quench you, so you will never be thirsty again."

"Okay, give me some so I won't have to keep coming here."

"Why don't you bring your husband here?" (A shift from physical thirst to spiritual thirst.)

"I don't have one." *Ooh that stung.* Avoiding her sex life, she shifts the topic to the controversy of where people should worship God.

But Jesus isn't deterred. "Yes, you tell the truth. You have had five husbands and now are living with someone."

Now, she is certain Jesus is a prophet of God. There is no other way he could have known this fact.

Jesus lays out the truth. "True worship is not a place. It's a person. I'm the One your people are waiting for. I'm the man."

Just then, the disciples returned with their lunch. Seeing Jesus conversing with a woman, the disciples dropped their mouths so wide you could have fit a whole sandwich in. Speaking to a woman of shady reputation and mixed race was definitely outside the norm for their day.

Embarrassed and exhilarated, she left her jar and ran to town exclaiming, "Come, see a man who told me everything I ever did. He's the Messiah!" Intrigued, the whole community poured out of the town gate and gathered to see Jesus (Jn. 4:29-30).

Simultaneously, Jesus tells the puzzled disciples now he's lost his appetite. They completely missed his point. Jesus declared that doing God's will satisfied him more than filling his stomach (Jn. 4:34).

So enthralled by Jesus' words, the townspeople asked him to stay longer. He stayed. And many believed.

Jesus cares for those of us who feel the least loved and respected. Despite Jesus' knowledge of the Samaritan woman's sin, he sought to meet her deepest need. He treats us with the same compassion.

Jesus' love and forgiveness are more refreshing than a cold drink on a hot day and more satisfying than a man in bed.

No matter what your history, no matter where you look for satisfaction, a relationship with Jesus is the better choice. Knowing him is our ultimate experience. And who knows, Jesus could use your changed life (like this Samaritan woman), to bring salvation to your friends and family.

> But when the kindness and love of God our Savior appeared, he saved us, not because of righteous things we had done, but because of his mercy. He saved us through the washing of rebirth and renewal by the Holy Spirit whom he poured out on us generously through Jesus Christ our Savior, so that having been justified by his grace, we might become heirs having the hope of eternal life (Titus 3:4-7).

A Woman Caught in Adultery

Angry, loud voices exploded into the air, filling an outdoor court room with malicious Pharisees and teachers of the law versus Jesus. They baited him with this question: Did the scantily dressed woman having been ripped from an adulterous bed, deserve stoning, a cruel, painful death? (Seifert, 2014)

They wanted to trap Jesus, testing him to see whether he was righteous under the law of Moses which they deemed their mark of true spirituality. The woman caught in the crossfire, certain of death, held her breath.

Jesus bent and wrote on the ground with his finger.

The atmosphere thickened with hatred as the men barraged him with more questions, seeking an excuse to kill him.

Jesus didn't care to save his reputation but sought to save this woman's life.

He addressed the men; "If any of you is without sin, let him be the first to throw a stone" and stooped again and wrote in the dirt (John 8:7). Jesus' act of physically lowering himself de-escalated the contentious scene. (I remember attending a Dan Allender's conference for abused women. After he spoke, he sat on the stage. His act of lowering himself neutralized the setting, enabling me and others to approach him.)

While Jesus doodled, one by one, each man left like a dog with its tail between its legs (Jn. 8:10).

Wrapping her garment tighter around her form, she glanced in Jesus' direction. He could throw the first stone. But he stood and faced her.

"Where did they go? Has anyone accused you?"

"No one."

"Neither do I. Go, and sin no more."

I don't know about you, but that kind of grace blows me away. Though Jesus acknowledged the woman's sin, he didn't allow the men to wedge her between them and him.

You can be assured of this, that when men have done evil against you, have even threatened to kill you, Jesus will one day judge them and set you free. Whatever state you find yourself in, it doesn't matter how you got where you are today. When you come before the mercy of Jesus, he washes you and clears your record (Col. 2:13).

> Do you not know that the wicked will not inherit the kingdom of God? Do not be deceived: Neither the sexually immoral nor idolaters nor adulterers nor male prostitutes nor homosexual offenders

nor thieves nor the greedy nor drunkards nor slanderers nor swindlers will inherit the kingdom of God. And that is what some of you were. But you were washed, you were sanctified, you were justified in the name of the Lord Jesus Christ and by the Spirit of our God (1 Cor. 6:9-11).

Jesus came into the world to save sinners... to show mercy and to display his unlimited patience (1 Tim. 1:15-16).

A Woman Criticized by Men

When a sinful woman heard Jesus was dining at Simon the Pharisee's home, she hurried and brought along an expensive bottle of perfume (Lk. 7:37-50).

As guests filled their stomachs with sumptuous food and wine, the host glared in disgust and murmured. Why would a woman like this be touching Jesus? And why would Jesus let her touch him if he was really God? (Lk. 7:39).

The woman, weeping over Jesus' mercy over her sin, took her hair and bent to wipe Jesus' wet feet, kissing them. As she poured perfume on Jesus' feet, the guests inhaled the sweet fragrance filling the house.

Deeply moved by this woman's act of love, Jesus told Simon a story. "A financier cancelled the debts of two people who owed him money. One owed five hundred denarii and the other fifty." Jesus asked, "Who would love him more?" (The debt was around five weeks of pay compared to a year and a half's pay.)

"The one who owed him more."

Jesus turns and looks directly at the woman but speaks to Simon. "You've been a poor host! And your attitude stinks! You didn't kiss me, wipe my feet, or pour oil on my head, but she's lavished me with kisses and perfume. Her multitude of sins have been forgiven." (In that day, it was common to kiss a guest, wipe their feet, and give them oil for their bodies.) Jesus not only criticized Simon for his inattentiveness, but declared him a self-righteous prig, ignorant of his own sin.

Turning, Jesus speaks tenderly to the woman, "You are forgiven. Your faith has saved you; go in peace" (Lk. 7:50).

The guests marveled not over the amazing food, but over Jesus' extravagant forgiveness of this woman's shady past.

Are we clueless of our sin (like Simon), or overcome by Jesus' lavish love and forgiveness? He willingly accepts our tears of repentance. Close your eyes and talk to him. Let Jesus fill you with himself, like the aroma of a lily.

> With my mouth I will greatly extol the Lord; in the great throng I will praise him. For he stands at the right hand of the needy one, to save his life from those who condemn him (Ps. 109:30-31).

Jesus and Our Response

Jesus reveals his depth of love to women. Let's muse for a moment. These women didn't have perfect childhoods. Who knows, maybe they came from abusive homes or had absent fathers. Jesus' counter-cultural behavior changed their lives through God the Father's merciful love.

God wants a relationship with you. Whether you've had a minimal religious background or thrown religion away, consider this: God's love for you is bountiful and unlimited.

As I vetted Jesus, he passed my test. I saw the tenderness in which he spoke to women. My heart connected to the compassion he felt for women in need, and my spirit felt overwhelmed by his defense for women who were overpowered by men. It boggled my mind. He never used women to benefit himself, but instead recognized their deeds and cared for their needs. I found Jesus to be completely trustworthy.

By now you likely have formulated an opinion about Jesus. What do you think of him? With which woman above do you identify? How did Jesus' response to her impact you?

Every woman has a little girl who combats within her. We need to redefine her. Jesus is more than trustworthy to calm her.

CHAPTER ELEVEN

Little Girls in Adult Bodies

A dead heart ...
and yet alive because it hurts.

A silent cry ...
to express a pain too great for words.

-Amy H.

A Suffering Woman

$\mathcal{D}$ o you remember the last time you were sick? What did it take to get better? How did your illness affect you or your family?

For over fifteen years, I have endured various chronic illnesses including fibromyalgia, adrenal fatigue, and myofascial pain syndrome. I've worked with a range of doctors and physical therapists to improve my fatigue, lower back pain, and pelvic floor. Thousands of dollars later, for which I am grateful to say God abundantly provided, I still struggle with pain.

Did you know there is a connection to your brain and pain? After six months of pain, even when it's removed, your brain will continue to send pain signals to your body. But there are some amazing new technologies to encourage healing due to the plasticity of our brain—therapies like biofeedback, Eye Movement

Desensitization and Reprocessing (EMDR), Cranial Sacral Therapy, Dynamic Neural Training System, and more. Sometimes thinking outside the box is necessary to get relief to calm your brain. I have used both holistic approaches and traditional approaches. I have a support group, a counselor, I do light exercise, and take supplements and meds (yes, that is allowed as a Christian). I read God's word. And I pray and sing. Sometimes loudly!

A few years ago, while strolling with my oldest granddaughter, Kirra, singing a butterfly song we made up together, I asked God, "Why are you allowing me to have this pain? What am I supposed to learn?"

At the entrance of our neighborhood, a gigantic cloud form floated above me of a strong man from the waist up. A thorny crown encircled his head and his muscular arms extended out and upward. I stood captivated in wonder. I heard (in my head) like the sound of thunder, "I Am the Lord God Almighty." The cloud-picture and simple message persuaded me to continue to trust God with my pain to this day.

Women need to grieve physical and emotional pain. For those of you who are fellow chronic pain sufferers, I know there is value in grieving the loss of *before-pain-me* to accept the *I-can't-function-me*. There's loss in losing your health. Living with illnesses such as Lymes or Lupus creates not only a mixture of feelings, but sometimes self-pity and resentment, or a feeling it's you against the world, or at least you versus all those healthy people out there. Cancer patients may undergo strenuous effects from radiation and chemotherapy and must process the emotional struggle of an unknown future.

Here are a few examples of women who grieve physical and emotional loss: "I'm frustrated because people can't see my pain or how much I'm battling," a chronic migraine sufferer said. "Inside

I'm on fire and filled with worry. I feel confused when brain-fog clouds my memory and conversations." Another sufferer said, "Pain dictates every decision I make. It's a part of every relationship I have. It's a constant and unwanted companion and cruel taskmaster."

Chronic sufferers are not the only people who suffer. Just so you don't feel left out, consider how women exhaust themselves from multi-tasking. We work, raise families, grieve over rebellious children, or addicted adult children, and care for elderly parents. Often, we slack off on self-care. Indeed, God designed and destined women with juggling-power, yet our bodies, minds, and souls need rest and healing.

A Dead Girl

This needed rest is also for girls and women who have suffered from sexual abuse. Here is an excerpt from a survivor of child sexual abuse, Cynthia Sutherland, in her book *Letters to my Brown Girls*. As an adult, she wrote a letter to herself when she was young:

> "Dear little brown princess, …I know, you feel sad most of the time. Let's talk about *why* you feel sad. If you don't want to talk. It's okay. I can wait until you are ready.
>
> Your body has what adults call private parts… Someone touching or putting anything into your private parts is *not* normal. The things Uncle did to your private parts were not normal. He was wrong each time he touched your private parts and pushed his penis into your vagina. The things he did were called sexual abuse….
>
> Talking about what he did to you will make you feel better because once you tell someone, they will stop him from hurting you. If you tell someone and he *still* hurts you, you should tell a different person. You should keep telling someone until he

stops hurting you. When he stops hurting you, the pain will stop and you will feel better." (Sutherland, 2022, pp.39-40)

Little abused girls grow up to be big girls. And we expect grown girls to be mature women, but often we are merely like the walking dead, doing what is expected of us. We carry a little-girl, big-girl complex. Let me tell you a secret. We all carry a bag of dead, remnant parts of our past. I believe God has a message for us.

A Suffering Woman

A woman, bleeding for twelve years, was approaching the crowd. Ladies, imagine being on your period for twelve years. The agony. I think I would shrivel up and die.

Penniless after seeing many doctors, her condition grew worse. In her day, bleeding identified her as unclean. Think of the me-against-them-mentality.

She was desperate for wholeness.

If she could touch Jesus' garment, she believed all would be well and could leave without notice. (Back in that day, there was a superstition that healing power could transfer to clothes.) (Wessell, 1984)

Picture an aerial scene with Jesus scuffling in a sweaty-smelling crowd with goats, sheep, and other tag-alongs.

Think. In. Slow. Motion.

Through the dusty air, the woman slides a hand in and feels a linen portion of Jesus' clothes.

Her bleeding ceased.

Relief spread through her body as energy escaped Jesus' body.

"Who touched my clothes?"

His disciples said, "Man, everybody and their brother!"

Jesus' seeking gaze brought the woman forward (yikes, not her plan). Trembling before the crowd in child's pose, she told Jesus of the bleeding, the doctors. The whole deal.

Imagine how she felt in front of this crowd. What must the crowd be thinking of her?

Jesus said, "Daughter, your faith has healed you. Go in peace and be freed from your suffering" (Mk. 5:34). The word Jesus used for healed is "sesoken," which means saved, meaning her healing was spiritual, not just physical. Jesus forgave her sins. (Wessell, 1984)

Jesus publicly acknowledged and reinstated this suffering woman to the watching crowd: "Receive this daughter of mine. Stop rejecting her. She's clean."

Imagine what this meant for her. No longer a social outcast. No longer in miserable physical pain. She had a new energy for living.

What would it mean for you to be welcomed into Jesus' family and to be called Daughter? How could your life be different to know you are chosen and to have a place called home?

Another Dying Girl

Meanwhile, a twelve-year-old-girl lay sick in bed after her father and mother had done everything to make her well. When her illness turned grave, Jairus, her father and a synagogue ruler, panicked and went searching for Jesus. Falling at his feet, he pled, "Come quickly. Save my daughter!"

Jesus agreed and they went.

Just as Jesus pronounced "Daughter," men appeared on the scene saying Jairus' daughter was dead. "Don't bother the teacher." Jairus' heart sunk to his toes. *Jesus stopped for the other crisis with the bleeding woman and now there's no hope for my daughter.*

Knowing his thoughts, Jesus said, "Don't be afraid. Just believe."

Greeted by weeping wailers, Jesus said, "Why all this commotion and crying? The child is not dead but asleep." Their cries changed to laughter, so Jesus dismissed them.

Inside, the room fell silent while Peter, James, and John stood to the side. The walls groaned alongside the mother and Jairus who looked on their motionless child.

Now, Jesus approached the child and gently lifted her by the hand, "Little girl, I say to you, get up!" (Mk. 5:41). And she did. She walked around. Jesus told her parents to give her something to eat.

The Little Girl in Us

How can these stories bring us healing and hope? First, consider the little girl of your past. When you were twelve, where did you live? Where did you go to school? Were your parents together? How did you get along with your siblings and friends? How did you spend birthdays and holidays?

Now, think about the little girl *inside you*. What were your likes and dislikes? Did you have freedom to express your ideas or opinions? What (or who) scared you? How did you feel about your body? What were your secrets?

One More Thought

As I've studied this passage, I'm intrigued by two details. We learn the girl was twelve-years old, and the bleeding woman suffered for twelve years. Jesus freed the woman from her years of suffering, which was the exact age of this girl. Could God redeem a weary woman and awaken the dead girl within her?

I believe the answer is yes! Jesus raised the voiceless, insecure girl in me. Jesus hears your cry and calls to you, "Little girl, wake up. Little Girl, WAKE UP!"

True Story

This story pierces my heart as I relive an event that happened to Jim and I twelve years ago, while at a conference in Florida. We received a late night call from our local hospital stating our sixteen-year old son Andrew was in critical condition following a car accident.

We fell to the floor in great suffering and weeping. We called our daughters to go to the hospital while we waited for a morning flight.

During the night, we got a call saying our son died.

Twelve agonizing hours later, we arrived at the hospital and finally set eyes on our son. Our hearts beheld his young face with sadness and disbelief. Though Jesus didn't choose to raise our son, I have the certain hope Andrew believed Jesus, and that one day we will be reunited.

Imagine yourself as a parent grieving over the dying, abused part of you. Jesus weeps with you. He gently calls your name to wake the sleeping dead girl or boy, man or woman. Even you.

Hard-Wiring

According to Jean Piaget, who's known for his theory on cognitive development, at the age of twelve we begin to reason, problem-solve, and think outside of ourselves. It's a time when we decide who we are, how we act, and what we believe. During this critical stage, the messages that come from our experience in relationships get hard-wired. Not just in our heads, but in our hearts.

We carry these shameful messages around like a teenager with an unplanned pregnancy. The lies swell within us like a womb full of shame. When the pain of these messages contract with force, we labor and deliver our little girl, so a new message comes forth.

One of the hard-wired messages I painfully birthed was my slut image. God replaced it with the image of a rose, through the help of a man named Paul.

What message have you labored to deliver?

A Rose

After three years living in France, my husband and I returned to the states seeking direction for our future. We met with a dear couple, Paul and Sandy from our mission in France, who counseled and prayed with us. Paul had been an angry person, but Jesus' forgiveness softened him into a kind and tender man. Sandy was a nurse and natural comforter. Since they felt safe, I told them about my-almost-rape experience. Paul's words reached deep into my soul.

"You're like a rose, an ever-unfolding beauty."

A what? Me, a rose? Fourteen years after that hostage-like weekend, I still felt dirty and fearful. *Lovely? Fragrant?* I couldn't imagine my heart unfold with naked vulnerability.

Yes. I wanted that. How I needed to unfold and let go.

With the rose image still in my mind, before heading back to the airport, I asked Jim to stop at a Home Goods store. I headed straight for the China section and to my delight, I found a teacup called, 'Old Country Roses' embellished with red, yellow, and pink roses.

Returning to France, I imagined unfolding like a rose. Sipping on a cup of Earl Grey, I pictured myself like the lovely, soft roses on my teacup. *I'm not a slut, I'm beautiful like a rose.* This truth pattered in my heart like a light spring rain. For the first time, I felt a renewal from the inside out.

This rose image reminds me how unwanted sexual experiences affect our openness. For instance, we may hesitate to open up in groups, or express our beauty in our clothing, or refrain from creative projects, or take time for self-care. A rose is beautiful, but you don't know how beautiful it is until it opens. Watching a rose bud unfold is a process. The layers of petals unfold one by one. But if it stays closed as a bud, a rose never achieves its full beauty and fragrance—its full potential as a flower.

Time passed, and as I learned this message of unfolding into my trust of God, the brittle dead petals of my untrusting attitude fell from my heart. I chose to embrace the soft beautiful, delicate petals inside. Like a rose, I unfolded, at least for that moment, and relaxed. It was healing relief. Little by little, intimacy with my husband grew sweeter. Over time, I didn't shame myself for mistakes. I practiced unfolding emotionally and letting go. Resting. Believing God was my loving father.

The rose image gave me hope. What image might help you find rest?

Books, Bunnies, and Lavender

"If you could imagine a feeling of peace, what would that be?" I asked a young woman who had come for counseling. She shifted her position on the couch, twisted her lip and looked at the ceiling.

"What I would imagine," Andrea (not her real name) said, "would be to sit next to Jesus, with my back against a tree, by a quiet river, enjoying a novel together." She loved books and the thought of sharing one in the presence of Jesus brought her rest. She opened up.

Andrea was abused on a school bus sharing a comic book with a schoolboy. Her choice to trust Jesus with her painful story brought her peace.

I love what God gave another woman when I asked her the same question. Susan (not her real name) sat quiet. Then said, "Lavender. It's fresh and clean." Susan felt free of disgusting smells that reminded her of her abuse. Her body and mind came to rest and she felt at peace.

God gave me another symbol for rest in my pet angora bunny, Peluche (pe-loosh), which means stuffed animal in French. My neighbor Maddie nicknamed him Lulu. I enjoyed playing with him in my family room. His soft pink ears and blue eyes appeared story-bookish, with a lock of white hair falling over his forehead. Lulu had a sweet and playful disposition, and would dance in a figure-eight pattern between my feet. Cocking his head to one side, he made a little run, leaped into the air, and clapped his back legs together. Then, he'd nestle between my legs sitting on the floor, and I'd bury my nose between his velvety warm ears and kiss him a dozen times, while he sat perfectly still. I transferred this bunny connection to myself; I imagined believing in my beauty and feeling safe in my body.

This sweet affection symbolizes how God desires intimacy with us. He wants us to feel his emotional warmth and physical comfort. Ask God to give you a physical symbol or mental picture with which you can use to process rest.

A Loving Father

Little girls need a loving father. In the story of the little girl, Jairus symbolizes the love of the heavenly Father who pursues us. Jairus loved his daughter so much that he risked his reputation going to Jesus for help.

In love, God pursued us by sending his Son Jesus to earth to live, die and rise again, forgiving us of the debt we owe him. If we believe in Jesus, we become his daughters and are welcomed into his family (2 Cor. 4:13-15).

Unfolding - *Recovering Your Identity After Sexual Intrusion*

If you put your hand over your heart, what would you say to the little girl in you? What does she need? Who does she need? Let me share four responses you may want to consider.

1. Recognize you are a wounded little girl. Let the adult you care for the little girl *in* you. You may find a friend or a counselor to listen to your story.

2. Seize a spirit of urgency. Time is of the essence in a crisis. With the energy Jairus pursued Jesus, what would you need to do or let go of to follow Jesus?

3. Put your faith in God's love. Only a little faith is needed. As Jesus lovingly searched for the suffering woman, he searches for you. You are not just one of a crowd. *You are the one he's pursuing in the crowd.*

4. Tell Jesus your story. The suffering woman told Jesus her whole truth. What will you tell Jesus? Talk to him honestly about your past and present.

CHAPTER TWELVE

Becoming a Daughter

> Hush, little child of mine
> in my arms, in my arms
> you will find love—
> love abiding, love unending,
> I give you my love.
>
> –Emily

In the movie series *Anne of Green Gables*, a red-haired orphan girl becomes part of a loving family. Even though the trip from the orphanage to her new home was brief, it took months and years to grow into a loved daughter. Like us, she had insecurities and struggles and unpleasing behaviors. It took time for Anne to trust Matthew and Marilla Cuthbert, and as she came to know their love, she relaxed, grew, and matured. What does it look like for us to grow as daughters in a relationship with a loving Father? What are the challenges we face as we learn to trust him?

Becoming Daughters

A daughter of God must wrestle with their question, *why did he allow this pain?* The only way to make sense of abuse is understanding that God wants to take our pain and use it for something good.

In love, God created Adam and Eve, the first humans, with the ability to make their own choices. And thus, sin came into the world. We have inherited this sin nature meaning we are naturally bent towards sin; the "we" includes our offenders *and* ourselves! Each of us has turned our own way (Is. 53:6). As difficult as it is, we must take our focus off our offender and look to what truth says. We all fall short of God's perfection (Rom. 3:23). But thankfully, God loved us, while we were against him (Rom. 5:8).

Jesus is the one who died in our place. When we trust his payment for our sin in our heart, and tell God we want to follow him, we are saved from our sin. This means letting go of being the stage director of our lives. Remember Carrie Underwood's song, *Jesus Take the Wheel*? Surrendering your way is a death of sorts. Faith in Jesus means we transfer self-trust to God-trust. We leave the dark and walk in his light.

Receiving forgiveness is the act of becoming a daughter. If you believe, he will receive you and call you daughter (Rom. 10:8). If you would like to become God's daughter, you could say something like this:

> Father, I believe you love me and have a purpose for my life. I believe you sent your Son, Jesus, to suffer on the cross in my place for my sins. Forgive me of my sins and doing life my way. I believe you rose again and have freed me from sin and guilt. Fill me with your Spirit to live as a daughter with you in control. I place my trust in you. Thank you for your peace and for eternal life. Amen.

This prayer is about the response of your heart. There are no prescribed words. You can simply say, "Lord, I believe!"

Daughters Are Welcome

When we believe in Jesus, we become daughters in God's family, born into a spiritual family of love (Eph. 2:9). God's love and welcome into his family changes our identity.

Jesus takes us, his daughters, pain and all, from the position of outsiders and makes us insiders. Outsiders live like orphans trekking through life without the provision and guidance of parents. When we trust Jesus, we receive a loving Father who has a plan to prosper us. "For I know the plans I have for you," declares the Lord, "plans to prosper you and not to harm you, plans to give you hope and a future" (Jer. 29:11-14).

We have a heavenly Father. Loving. Interested. Involved. Being God's daughter means we are accepted and cared for like an adopted child. My friends Chuck and Lisa adopted their daughter Mikaela from birth over ten years ago. Watching them welcome her into their home modeled to me how God welcomes us into his family. I love how they celebrate her birthdays with creative activities such as treasure hunts and horseback riding.

What difference does belonging to God's family make in your life? Imagine God celebrating you in his family. What could change in your life if you decided to join God's family?

Privileges of a Family

In God's family, a daughter has protection. Since Jesus conquered death, he protects us from death. Eternal separation from a loving God is the ultimate punishment for our sins. Jesus' death cancelled the penalty of our sin and final destination (Col. 2:13-14). Instead, we receive his righteousness (2 Cor. 5:21).

A daughter has provision. God will help us with our earthly needs, but more importantly he gives us the hope of eternal life.

Ephesians 1 tells us we have an inheritance. We get to live in God's presence rather than spend our lives in hell separated from God's love. This eternal life will be indescribable. In fact, Romans 8:18 tells us that our current sufferings can't be compared with the glory and beauty that awaits us in heaven.

Being a daughter means we hold onto God's promises. God doesn't promise he will keep us from pain. He promises he will never leave us alone in the pain (Heb. 13:5). He promises he will hear us when we cry. We can never go anywhere without his presence (Ps. 139:7-10). He promises he will work all things unpleasant (this means the pain we've endured, even abuse or harassment), for our good and for his glory (Rom. 8:28). God can use the effects of abuse for some good purpose.

What privilege most attracts you as a daughter in Christ?

How Daughters Live

Living as a daughter of Christ means freedom, but also surrender. How could this be so? Since Jesus bought us with his blood, in gratefulness we offer ourselves to him. At times, it feels like dying. The writer of Romans said our lives are living sacrifices (Rom. 12:1-2). This is how we please God.

Let's consider the adulterous woman who surrendered illegitimate relationships with men when Jesus intervened in her impending death (by men). The minority woman willingly surrendered her reputation to an entire community when Jesus met the longing of her heart. The sinful woman surrendered to Jesus' compassion in the midst of critics. The bleeding woman died to her fear of being publicly exposed in place of Jesus' relational interest in her.

I remember the day in middle school when I decided to surrender my will to Jesus' will. Distraught by the gossip and backbiting of friends, I picked up my books in science class where the cool group sat and walked across the room and sat with a group of Christians. My new friends welcomed me, but I imagined my old friends throwing darts at my back. This time I didn't care. I had the acceptance and unconditional love of my new friends and God.

A Daughter's Transformed Thinking

As winter snow melts into spring, so Jesus transforms our faulty thinking. His loving kindness softens our self-hatred as the earth softens and prepares for spring. The lies we believe are rendered powerless. A new way of life blossoms within us. The Word gives us the truth about who are. We are created and chosen by him (Rev. 4:11; Eph. 1:11). We have worth in His eyes. God says:

you are worthy and wanted,

you belong,

you're seen,

you're important,

you're pure,

you're beautiful,

you're clothed,

you're perfect,

you will grow.

But just as it takes a season to plant a new truth, it takes a season to grow. We need patience like a farmer to watch and wait for God (Jam. 5:7).

A Heart at Rest

Knowing I'm a loved daughter means I don't have to overwork in vain. The position of my heart is at rest. Relaxed. Trusting. Open. When we rest in the love of Jesus, we become beautiful women.

This resting stance has no fear. And it doesn't fade with age or clothes that go out of style (1 Pet. 3: 1-7). Inner rest is the opposite of control and manipulation.

Resting in your new identity will give you a new power to change like the eagle. Isaiah 40:31 says, "but those who hope in the Lord will renew their strength. They will soar on wings like eagles; they will run and not grow weary, they will walk and not be faint."

As we learn to rest in our identity as daughters, the enemy will constantly accuse us day and night (Rev. 12:10). His lies may cause us to shut down like a rose bud. Let's talk about triggers that touch us uncomfortably and how to combat them. God will empower us to move from rose bud to a rose in full bloom.

PART THREE

New Power

CHAPTER THIRTEEN

Triggers and Trauma

> Let go of my sword,
> let go of being strong,
> feel my terror,
> tightness,
> rapid breathing...
> I scream.

One simmering day in August, Danielle invited a friend and her kids over to play. She broke out in a cold sweat when her daughter came inside from the neighbor's with a cowboy hat, pistol, and dangling handcuffs from her wrist. "Where did you get those things? You are not to play with them again. Do you hear me?" Danielle confided in me that as a teenager, her boyfriend used handcuffs on her during unwanted sexual acts. This trigger caused an explosive reaction.

In *Emotionally Healthy Spirituality*, Peter Scazzero describes triggers like an emotional allergy which he defines as "an intense reaction to something in the present that reminds us, consciously or unconsciously, of an event from our history."

Triggers are those events or exchanges with people that bring us an overwhelming sense of emotion. A trigger may occur at an unexpected time. One moment you are coasting through your day and the next moment ushers you back to your assault, date rape, or traumatic childhood.

If you've been abused, you will likely experience triggers. High anxiety and traumatic stress will likely follow a trigger, so learning coping skills to regain a state of calm is essential in the healing process.

Triggers come in seasons of life and especially during transitions when we feel most vulnerable. For instance, when women start a family, their past abuse can rouse them to protect their children. A woman shared with me how her stepfather molested her as a child and when she was a teenager, he exposed himself while using explicit language.

When she got married, she projected negative feelings towards her husband when he set negative but normal boundaries with their children. At times, she inappropriately intervened between her kids and her husband, with an irrational need to protect them when they were not in danger. Since her mother didn't protect her from her stepdad's abuse, this caused irrational fears for her own children's safety. She also felt uncomfortable in her sexual relationship with her husband. This nearly destroyed her marriage. Thankfully she got help in counseling to address her triggers. I'm so grateful her marriage is intact. Currently, she works with kids who have endured trauma. What an example of the power of working through triggers.

Survivors remember their abuse in various seasons. Even the change of weather or a specific holiday can remind survivors of their abuse. My heart stirs with anxiety in autumn and during football games, especially homecoming games. The blow of a referee's whistle, the band, cheerleaders, and orange clothes inflict me with shallow breathing and remind me of the helplessness I felt. At such times, I imagine Jesus holding my hand in the crowd, and it helps me calm down. Grounding myself in the current moment reminds me it's all over. It's not going to happen again.

When we identify our thoughts, feelings, and longings during the distress of a trigger, we can regain a stance of rest based on the comfort and assurance we have as daughters in Christ. Our goal is to remind ourselves of the truth so we can move beyond the fearful feelings.

What is one particular truth you learned about triggers that you can apply to your life? How does this help you understand someone else?

Triggers and Shame

Shame is one emotion that our triggers cause. Shame is both an emotion and the belief that we are faulty human beings compared to everyone else. The devil delights when we sit in a seat of shame, (like a naughty chair in the principal's office). Ridding yourself of shame requires moving into it. It's uncomfortable, but it's healthy and necessary.

If you can put words to what brings you shame, you are on your way to freedom. Let me illustrate. Pretend you have a coin to represent your heart where one side is shame, and the other side is desire. When we move into our shame, we naturally discover our desire underneath the pain.

Our desire steers us into our heart's longings. We long to be filled with love, to belong, to be seen and heard. God has given us these desires. He longs to tell us we have great worth. We're beautiful. God sees an unblemished daughter before him. He longs to satisfy our desires with himself.

Jesus took our burden of shame. He scorned the shame of the cross. Hebrews 12:2 says, "Let us fix our eyes on Jesus, the author and perfecter of our faith, who for the joy set before him endured the cross, scorning its shame, and sat down at the right hand of the throne of God."

Jesus' resurrection proves he canceled the effects of shame. His position seated next to God proves it. We have the same position. If Jesus lives in us by the Holy Spirit, we have Jesus' power. What a significant truth. Rather than debilitating shame, the love and grace of Jesus rests on us. With our new identity, we have a new heart and new motivation.

From what burden of shame can Jesus free you?

Identifying Triggers

Let's talk about a few triggers. After my assault, when I saw gray-haired men, adrenaline rushed through my veins. For instance, my body felt a strong magnetic pull. My mind and body replayed the danger I felt with Mike. Anxiety and guilt flooded me. I believed the lie that I was flirting. *I attracted him, it was my fault, of course.*

When a trigger hits, we must reposition our identity. My brain categorized every gray-headed man as a power-hungry molester. I used grounding techniques to discern and interpret the situation. If I saw a gray-haired man at church, I reminded myself he was not Mike. And, after all, I was at church, not in the middle of his castle apartment. And I had to give myself credit. I had learned a few things since the assault. I learned to listen to my gut. I stayed close to my husband in social settings or told him when I felt uncomfortable with a certain man. This helped me relax and learn to lessen my reactive responses.

To further illustrate, when Jim and I attended school for our counseling degree, we borrowed a book from one of our classmates. As Clay handed me the book, electric-like waves pulsed in through the book from his hand to my hand to my chest. Shock, tension, guilt, and pleasure jumbled like a food processor inside me.

I had only borrowed a book, but guilt tormented my brain as if I had committed adultery. I chalked it up to one more unbearable interchange with a man. But a new day was coming. I had work to do, for I had not yet grieved my abuse. I longed to experience an interchange with a man that felt healthy and normal.

Identifying triggers takes time. Susan recalls playing unattended for hours with her stepsister. Years later when making love with her husband, certain positions induced anxiety. In counseling, she identified this trigger by remembering the visits at her father's house. She recalled her stepsister imitating sex scenes with her that she'd seen on television. The memory evoked butterflies swirling in her stomach as she recollected unpleasant odors. Once she identified this trigger, Susan permitted herself to stop and calm herself during intimacy with her husband. Acknowledging the trigger allowed her to regain a sense of peace. Afterward, she could open up to her own sexual desire and was able to refocus her attention on her husband. The process is slow work, but don't be discouraged. You will grow.

When you think about the trigger images you just read, what comes to mind? Perhaps there are certain experiences causing anxiety for you, but you are unaware of the link between this experience and a prior experience. Reflect. Can you connect what you feel in the present to a similar feeling in your past?

The Brain and Trauma

When a person experiences trauma or violence, such as someone getting injured in an accident or war or through sexual intrusion (often associated with rape, sexual abuse, or assault), their brain absorbs and stores the experience. People who have experienced such events may develop a reaction that debilitates them from living a meaningful life called post-traumatic stress disorder or PTSD. (NIHM, 2019) An understanding of what happens in the brain will aid us in the healing process. However, this is a simplistic explanation, as I don't want to get too techie.

The brain of someone with PTSD appears structurally and functionally different. The volume in the brain actually diminishes. Our brain helps regulate our emotions. Survivors of traumatic events struggle to calm themselves when a stimuli associated with their previous trauma is introduced. Thankfully, human brains can be re-wired with medication and therapy to increase the volume of their brains. (Wlassoff, 2015)

You can appreciate the reason why survivors want to avoid anything that reminds them of their abuse. (Wlassoff, 2015) Consequently, this reduces one's ability to distinguish between the past and the current moment. Survivors of abuse can become stressed significantly with a stimuli from the past, such as watching a movie or looking at a photo, or hearing words or sounds that remind them of the traumatic event. (Wlassoff, 2015)

Our brain has an area that helps us process emotions, especially the emotion of fear. In trauma this part of our brain gets activated. People with PTSD can become so stricken with fear that even a slightly associated stimuli can cause anxiety, panic, flashbacks, and hyperarousal. (Wlassoff, 2015). Facing our fear lends us the opportunity to loosen its hold.

We can retrain the brain to diminish this hyperarousal state. This is called post-traumatic growth. (Debiec, 2018) The promise of hope in healing from traumatic memories comes not through avoidance, but rather exposure. However, in the grieving process, one important factor is to ensure there is a safe environment with low levels of stress. Looking into our past, and releasing those events, could lead to re-traumatization. See the appendix for a list of techniques that will assist you if you should experience hyperarousal. If you have continued problematic hyperarousal, you should stop and wait to re-enter those memories or get help from a counselor.

The good news for those who've been traumatized by unwanted sexual intrusion is that the brain can unlearn to be afraid. A study was made showing how the brain lights up in similar areas when one experiences something or imagines it. If you imagine something you fear in a safe environment the brain's response to fear can be minimized. The greater your imagination the greater the brain potentially changes. (ScienceDaily, 2018)

Let me share an example of retraining the brain. Think of any situation that creates anxiety in you. Picture Jesus and imagine what he would do and say. Joy, who was abused by several men, imagined Jesus during a state of hyperarousal. In her imagination, she invited Jesus to the dinner table where, as a young girl, she was banned for being naughty. Fear and anxiety turned to smiles and peace as she described talking with Jesus. He invited her into his mansion where they sat eating strawberries and watermelon on paper plates. Her joy came not from the meal or simple place setting, but in the intimate conversation with a man who enjoyed spending time with her.

Where might you recognize trauma and hyper-arousal in your life? Imagine bringing Jesus' presence into that place and allow his presence to create safety and meaning. This may retrain your brain to not respond so negatively the next time you perceive a threat.

Your Body, Trust, and Triggers

In August of 2005, Hurricane Katrina ripped through the levees of New Orleans, causing over 1,200 deaths and overwhelming destruction. We call the survivors and those who didn't survive victims of a natural tragedy.

Like a hurricane, offenders bring devastation to their victims as an enemy who invades and occupies one's home. Their intrusion breaks our trust, the unseen levee between us and them.

Why is trusting that someone will honor our personal space important to an abuse survivor? As victims we need to re-establish safety and protection.

Developing good boundaries between you and your offender is like rebuilding a strong levee. This will promote a sense of empowerment. We must establish a sense of self-respect to restore personal space and safety. When you don't feel heard or free to make your own choices, this indicates a power imbalance in a relationship. A power imbalance diminishes your ability to have a healthy equal relationship.

Learning to develop greater respect for yourself will lower the dominance you feel in relationships. Being assertive allows you to set boundaries, for example, by not letting people talk to you in a certain way and not catering to every request they have. In building self-respect between you and your offender you might decide to stop communication or limit your contact. If you do decide to meet with them, bring a friend with you. Yet, just as a levee protects a city, there are times when disaster strikes, so even with good boundaries set in place, an offender could try his best to manipulate, guilt, and control your life with catastrophic force. Keep making good choices based on self-respect and this will empower you.

Reflect on what is taking place in your relationships. Is there a healthy sense of balance? You are Jesus' daughter. Use your desire and dignity to make your relationships safer and more balanced. Let your decisions reflect your sense of worth and trust in Christ.

Self-Soothing After a Trigger

Triggers create crisis-like feelings. As a frightened garden lizard changes color, so a survivor in distress turns victim. The definition of victim is "a person harmed, injured, or killed as a result of a crime, accident, or other event or action. A person who is tricked or duped." ("Victim," n.d.)

A trigger has the power to set you off for periods of time—from minutes to months. Developing awareness of people and places which cause triggers helps one prepare and diminish the strength of a trigger.

In working with women who have experienced abuse, I've often watched how quickly a trigger overcomes them in the present. Sometimes, just being quiet in their presence while they cry helps them self-soothe. They know I'm there. I'm listening. Having a safe person present during a trigger can restabilize a troubled soul.

We can't always fully prepare for triggers or know when they'll occur. In life we engage in dozens of interchanges every day with people where we live, work, and play. It is essential to learn and use skills for out-of-control feelings that arise from triggers. You can use breathing techniques, muscle relaxation, guided imagery, music and grounding to bring yourself back to a place of calm.

Use the resource chapter on tools of expression, relaxation, and communication to identify your emotions. Is there an associated sound or smell with your trigger? What message comes to mind about you or the person who offended you?

Battle with Triggers

Three days ago I was taken in by a social security phone scam. The caller used deceit, intimidation, and threats to coerce me to disclose personal information. For days after that, I cancelled credit cards, changed banks, and added protective measures to ensure my identity protection.

The experience reminded me of my assault. Afterward, I lay weeping on my couch from fatigue, shame, and guilt. How was I so dumb? I wondered why God let this happen. What was he up to?

In response to my crisis, I processed it as I would an assault. In spite of my victimization, I refocused. I felt empowered by identifying the caller as the evil person. Though I felt deceived, I focused on Jesus. I admitted my disappointment in myself and let the Spirit strengthen me by his power. And I received comfort from my husband and friends who prayed for me.

This is how we battle abuse. Each trigger produces an opportunity to fight. God says, "Be strong and courageous. Do not be afraid or terrified because of them (triggers), for the Lord your God goes with you; he will never leave you nor forsake you" (Deut. 31:6, parentheses mine).

Holding onto the Word of God is like handling a sharp sword (Heb. 4:12). We use the word to disempower our enemy. "The Lord is my light and my salvation; whom shall I fear? The Lord is the stronghold of my life; of whom shall I be afraid?" (Ps. 27:1).

Using self-soothing tools, reading the Word, and making good decisions frees us from bondage and a victim mentality. As we heal, the time between battles will lengthen.

For example, this morning I had a totally unexpected trigger after a physical therapy appointment. The interior of the building was getting a make-over, and things were a bit disheveled. I asked the fellow at the front desk about my bill. "Sure," he said, checking the computer screen before him. "By the way, my beautiful wife standing behind me is working on the new renovations."

A slim blonde woman dressed in a gray shirt and yoga pants was discussing the renovation project with a worker. I answered, "Yeah renovations are exciting, but they can be stressful too." I walked out after the pleasant interchange, but felt uneasy as I drove to the grocery store afterward.

I replayed the conversation in my head. Why did that man say, "My beautiful wife?" Was it because I was tempting him and he wanted to draw his attention to her? Or did he want her to know she was beautiful, in case she thought he was looking at me? I felt shame, and confusion.

So, I had to do just what I'm telling you to do. Sitting in the parking lot, I sat quietly and reflected. Several years ago, I might have pined over this all day, ignoring the root of my feelings. I retracked what was said and remembered that I don't like getting caught between a man and his wife. It's what happened with Mike and Nan.

I reminded myself that the enemy was on my trail. I thought of the shield of faith. It's the armor piece that extinguishes the flaming arrows of the evil one. In faith, I told myself none of those thoughts were true about me. I am God's loved daughter and I wanted Jesus to show me his goodness. I wanted my heart to rest in him. So I said, "Get out of here, Satan. Your arrows are wet." I imagined drenching Satan's flames with a huge hose. Not a hint of smoke remained, only a pool of water. Nothing could fire me up any longer. The trigger lost its power. I went on about my day, not giving the scene a second thought.

Battling triggers is like leaping on a stone jutting from dangerous rapids to shore's safety. The battle is real; empower yourself with the Word. What is your steppingstone (trigger), and the leap of truth (belief) to reach the other side?

God's Word for Triggers

God's word powerfully stabilizes and sustains us when we feel anxious from a trigger. Search the Psalms or the book of Isaiah, for example, to find hope and comfort. Here are a few of my favorites: Psalm 118:6, "The Lord is with me; I will not be afraid. What can man do to me?"

"Fear not, for I have redeemed you; I have summoned you by name; you are mine" (Is. 43:1b). "Those who look to him are radiant; their faces are never covered with shame" (Ps. 34:5).

Uncovering triggers will bring more grief and mourning. So do a little self-care. Go for a walk. Take a hot bath.

Remember Jesus is loving and kind. He does not condemn you when a trigger hits your day. He is trustworthy. Jesus calls you Daughter. Satan is the loser.

Now that we have defined and identified triggers, let's consider how to fuel ourselves with the power to change.

CHAPTER FOURTEEN

Learning Assertiveness

> Weak men
> are posers
> wielding
> immeasurable
> damage.

When I moved to the foothills of the Asheville Mountains, nothing prepared me for the culture and triggers I experienced in Rutherfordton, a small rural town in the Bible belt, a land of good ol' boys where folks waved from their cars and where I swerved to miss roadkill hauling my kids to school. Don't get me wrong, I liked the friendliness of the south, but I had to adapt to southern men.

A few days after I moved, I discovered a small discount grocery store. Stuffing my bags in the back of my car, I saw a man sauntering towards me. My heart jumped to see a white-haired man dressed in scruffy overalls with a beard reaching to his waist. Pointing with his thumb at the next lot, he rattled about T-bone steak, fifty percent off. Nodding my head, I thanked him for this tip. Another time before Christmas, a sweet and desperate man in Walmart (the hub of life in town), approached me holding a pair of earrings in one hand and a bottle of perfume in another, and asked my opinion for a gift for his wife. I hesitated but pointed to one. Open dialogue between a southern man and a woman both unsettled me and relaxed my anxiety to know polite conversation didn't equal sexual intrusion.

But let me tell you about a time when I felt powerless around a man.

G-Man, An Insecure Man

Most women sense the difference between a man chitty-chatting about nothing (as the men in the above stories) and a man who flirts and gets under your skin. I had a provoking experience with a man who worked at a grocery store. A salt-and-pepper haired man with matching beard who wore wire-rimmed glasses stalked me for months. I'll call him G-man for grocery man.

His annoying attention started when he'd say hello from ten feet away. *Was he talking to me?* I'd wonder.

He trailed me regularly. He spied down the aisle while I browsed honey flakes and oat bran; another time he lurked around while I picked between cans of pineapple slices or chunks. As his attention increased, my stomach tensed. I pretended to check my list. *It's no use. I'm his target.*

I'd heap guilt on myself for being the dumbest lady in the store. I mean, I couldn't even tell him to bug off.

A week later, I watched him flirting with another woman. I fumed. He acted like a prey animal seeking a kill. But come on, how harmful could he be?

You're probably like me, I thought about G-man. *I could turn this around spiritually.* I was thinking I would witness to him. *That's what he needs, the Lord, not a woman.* I asked my husband to pray for me as G-man's attention started to arouse a desire in me. I did not want to imagine sex scenes in my mind. *Sigh.* I knew I was feeling the shame of the aftermath of sexual abuse.

One day G-man hovered near me at the meat section. The warmth of his presence threw me into a panic. Pointing to a hunk of tri-tip I said, "How w-would you cook this roast?"

"Awe, you can grill 't with a lit'l salt, pepper, olive oil and garlic, or you kin' put 't in the oven with a chimichurri sauce," he said.

Enlightened, I answered, "Well, that sounds good. Thank you." Of course, I failed to change the conversation to a spiritual topic and trotted away pushing my cart.

Before my next trip, I prayed to God for an opportunity. I wanted to bring up Jesus if I happened to see G-man. Sure enough, he walked right beside me while I moved towards the produce. What audacity. Paralysis took over my body as I checked whether the avocados were ripe and mashed them with my fingers.

Another failure.

For the third time, I prayed God would give me the strength to speak to G-man. Early in the morning, the store had few customers, and I welcomed the thinking space. My skin turned to goosebumps in the dairy section as I hovered over Greek yogurt with honey. An uneasy sense lifted my chin, and thirty feet away the only other person standing, was G-man. *Here's your chance, Lynne. He's right in front of you.* My feet froze to the linoleum. My heart hammered like a school fire-drill. *Open your mouth, Lynne! Say it. "I don't like your attention! What you really need is the love of a heavenly Father to satisfy your drive."*

G-man stood within my reach; I could have walked right up to him. But my body, weighted with emotional chains, remained bound. Once more, I walked out of the store with a heart grieving like the massive gray clouds looming in the sky.

Some time went by as I patronized other stores, avoiding the awkwardness of my failure. Finally, I couldn't get around it, and headed back to this grocery store. I prayed God would help me confront G-man. Walking past the cosmetics, I heard a familiar voice say, "Hel—lo."

Our eyes met and there stood three women who huddled with G-man!

"How you bin doin'?" he asked.

Clenching my fists, I glanced their way and wavered. *I could shred him to pieces right in front of these ladies!* But the voice inside me didn't budge. Straightaway, my legs formed a beeline for the paper goods.

I felt defeated. Utterly. Completely. Defeated. *Why couldn't I speak to him?* I had no clue. Wasted prayers. What would God think of me now?

I thought that I was damaged forever. Why would I still be so affected some twenty years after my abuse? It just didn't make sense to me. Why did anxiety dominate my life? There wasn't any real threat here, but I felt it. I couldn't even fight against an overfriendly man at a grocery store.

What part of this story do you connect with? Where would you draw the line between casual conversation with a man and when it crosses a line? No matter how many times you think you've failed, don't give up. God is for you.

God's Powerful Plan

God had a plan to encourage his people in their oppression. He also wants to save us and ransom us from our failures (like mine).

> Isaiah 51:11b-15 says, "…Gladness and joy will overtake them, and sorrow and sighing will flee away. (I need that.)

"I, even I, am he who comforts you. Who are you that you fear mortal men, (even perpetrators and stalkers) the sons of men, who are but grass, that you forget the Lord your Maker, who stretched out the heavens and laid the foundations of the earth, that you live in constant terror every day because of the wrath of the oppressor, who is bent on destruction? For where is the wrath of the oppressor? The cowering prisoners will soon be set free; (That's you and me, and victims-alike) they will not die in their dungeon, nor will they lack bread.

"For I am the Lord your God, who churns up the sea so that its waves roar—the Lord Almighty is his name. I have put my words in your mouth and covered you with the shadow of my hand—

"I who set the heavens in place, who laid the foundations of the earth, and who say to Zion, 'You are my people.'" (Italics mine).

God desires to comfort, free, and empower his people. What does that mean to you?

A New Perspective of Power

While nursing my profound sense of powerlessness, a couple of weeks later God gave me a new outlook watching the movie *The Wizard of Oz*.

The great and powerful Master of the land sends Dorothy and her friends through trials and tribulations to acquire the broom of the Wicked Witch of the West. As they approach the arena of the Wizard, lightning flashes, thunder peals, and a cloud of green smoke rises. A booming voice shakes them to the ground.

Dorothy's dog, Toto, jumps out of her arms, and with his jaws pulls aside a curtain revealing the back of a rather small white-haired man maneuvering a control panel, frantic and flustered.

Seeing this, Dorothy comes to her senses. Her voice strikes with venom. "You're nothing but a mean, bad wizard!"

The Wizard's face softens and his tone melts. He explains to Dorothy and her friends they already possess everything they've ever wanted. The Scarecrow had a brain, the Tinman had a heart, and the Lion had courage. Dorothy possessed the ability to go home, *if she believed.*

Empowering the Weakhearted

Watching Dorothy turn from being powerless to powerful helped me tap into my own fear. How I wanted to be empowered! When Dorothy saw the Wizard's faults and imperfections, she spoke! Weakness empowered her to change. Like the flick of a light-switch, I transferred the concept to myself.

Why, *I am an equal to those who formerly abused and intimidated me!* I could choose to look behind their veneer. I could choose to disempower my fear of male domination or intimidation (especially men in roles of authority). It bolstered my desire to believe that one day, I would stand up to a man who harassed me.

As the Wizard hid behind his curtain with the illusion of pomp and power, so a perpetrator hides in reputation and superiority (or his needy identity and hungry appetite). Abusers prey on needy and vulnerable people. Many perpetrators continue abusing for years until (or if) they are exposed. They lie safe in their positions, protected by their accomplices. But behind their intimidating facades, they are mere people too, no better than others.

What experiences of harassment or unwanted attention have you endured? What kind of power does your perpetrator still hold over you? Consider this, though you experienced shame and felt worthless and humiliated, in spite of the power imbalance between you and your offender, being made in God's image gives you dignity no matter what the offense against you. When you have Jesus living in you, you possess more power than your abuser.

When you believe in your sense of dignity, you can choose power over the offense done to you. You can reclaim what God has placed in you. "You, dear children, are from God and have overcome them, because the one who is in you is greater than the one who is in the world" (1 Jn. 4:4).

If you imagine yourself as equal to your abuser, what would that change for you? What could you say or do?

Getting Power From My Head to My Heart

But how does a victim of abuse use this power once they find it? I have a friend named Kathy, who happens to be a counselor. I told her about my woes of stalker G-man. I described, "In the moment I'm always afraid, and can't find the courage to get the words out of my mouth. I'm angry. *Afterward*, I can think of what to say, but then it's too late." Kathy directed me to a message by pastor Andy Stanley. So, I went online and pulled up a series of sermons which talked about confession. Eek. That sounded hard. He explained how telling a trusted person about the junk in our closets breaks the power of bondage in us. Wow, why hadn't I thought of that before?

After listening to Andy Stanley's messages, I called Kathy back. She said, "Why don't you start by confessing your fears to a man you trust?"

Phew, now that was going to be a risk of faith, but what a great idea. Confessing my fears to any man would feel like losing control, like I was in a chokehold. I decided I would approach my boss as I had an unhealthy fear of leaders.

I found this powerful scripture to help. "We have this hope as an anchor for the soul, firm and secure. It enters the inner sanctuary behind the curtain, where Jesus, who went before us, has entered on our behalf" (Heb. 6: 19-20a). An anchor can't be seen but digs deeply into the earth below fluid waters to hold a boat steady. Faith (like an anchor) is belief in the unseen. Faith pleases God. I had no strength of my own, but I believed God could give me his strength to make this confession. If Jesus' power could raise his dead body, he could give me supernatural strength to speak. Jesus was my anchor. My faith in his power would strengthen me to share my struggle with my boss.

I picked a day and plodded to my boss's office (of course to talk about something else). George's kind face and weathered skin (from years he spent in Alaska) met me with gentleness. His office was stuffed with souvenirs—a map, a soft sheepskin on the floor, and two snow-shoes resembling antique tennis rackets that hung on the wall. I placed my hands on my knees to steady and calm myself.

"George, I'd like to talk to you about something in my story. When I was in my young twenties, I was molested by a man much older than me. Recently, I've been working on breaking the power of that experience and by expressing this verbally to you as a man, it will help break the silence and re-empower me."

"Thanks for your courage and honesty, Lynne," he said. "Is there anything I can do to help you in this?"

A flood of relief swept over me like a kid on her last day of middle school. I had opened my dark closet to another man outside of my husband. *Deep sigh.* "Well, I think, if you ever see me looking nervous or uncomfortable, just ask me how I'm doing."

After that conversation, I felt more relaxed in his presence and those of the other men on staff. I took the risk, trusting Jesus would take care of me. And he did.

What about you? Speaking honestly about your fear could break the silence and power of your past. Something felt different and good inside me. It will for you too.

Breaking the Power

Though I never went to the grocery store to confront G-man, I used the strength I gained from practicing on my boss for another incident. It wasn't long before I used my voice in a live harassment situation. My husband and I were visiting a local church. An elderly man I'll call Mory greeted people at the door. In fact, before I could make my way into the sanctuary, I had to get through five male greeters (no kidding). Ugh, what exhausting work.

One night at a Bible Study, I heard Mory tell the group, "I like flirting with the young girls 'cause I'm older and can get away with it."

Well, my radar went up!

One Sunday, before leaving the house, I asked Jim to stay on my right side so he would protect me from Mory. Walking towards the doorway, Mory, chipper-like, thrust his hand out to Jim, "Good morning." Good. I've made it without an assault!

Just then, a hand gripped my elbow and yanked me. It was Mory. He looked at Jim, "Boy, you know how to pick a good-looking wife, don't ya?"

My heart shifted in high gear. I fumbled through the doorway up the carpeted aisle to find a seat. *He made a spectacle of me and passed it off as a compliment to Jim!* The band on stage strummed choruses and the words blurred on the screen. I knew unless I went and spoke my mind to this man, I couldn't worship.

I decided to speak to Mory and invited Jim to join me.

Thrusting my hands in my sweater pockets, I marched back down the aisle with my heart thumping and went straight for Mory.

I felt weak, but this time I was actively leaning on the power Jesus gave me. Quietly, but firmly I said, "I need to talk with you." My arms trembled and my voice drifted.

Jim tried to intervene for me. Renewing my energy, I interrupted, "This time I need to talk."

Mory's mouth hung loose and stood attentive to me.

"I was sexually abused by a Christian man in my twenties, and I feel uncomfortable when men give me compliments the way you did. I want you to stop." It wasn't exactly what I wanted to say, but he got the message.

Horizontal wrinkles appeared on his forehead as he placed one hand on his hip. With sincerity he said, "Well, I'm glad you told me."

Turning my back, I steadied myself walking to my chair. I felt like a hot mess but for the first time, I had thrown my anchor overboard and my weakness gave in to trust. Oh how feeble I was, but I felt the power of Jesus. Holding onto the chair in front of me, I joyfully sang every word of the next chorus. God conquered my enemy. A victory! I was weak, but he gave me strength.

As the last hymn finished, out of my left eye, I sensed a movement near Jim. Mory stood with his head bowed. Placing his hand on Jim's shoulder, looking us in the eyes, he said, "I want to tell you both today, I respect that you came and talked with me. Sometimes, I can be a little cavalier. I'm sorry, and I want you to know (this time he turned to me) that God used you to minister to me today."

I stood emboldened. God's power enabled me to speak to a man who had harassed me.

How about you? Have you had any Morys in your life? Could you ask God to show you how being weak might be a predecessor to trusting in his power? Is there someone you need to confront?

Even when we grow in our ability to use our voice there are circumstances when God allows a spiritual battle and we feel tempted. The struggle is intended to take us deeper in our growth.

CHAPTER FIFTEEN

When the Enemy Attacks

Sitting in the shadows
alone with my shame, guilt, and tears
but not invisible, my Heavenly Father saw and knew every detail
He understood my deepest heart's desire and fear that day
to come and cry freely in His loving arms

-Emily

Have you ever prayed for one thing and received something quite different? One Monday morning, I spent time praising and singing to get insight for my writing. In the privacy of my office I made up a song and danced to God.

On Wednesday, after receiving a medical massage, my body winced in pain. I had hoped it would give me some relief. During the massage there were times when the therapist seemed unprofessional in how he touched me and it felt awkward, however, I didn't say anything in the moment. Later that day I felt lingering discomfort and ambivalence about what had happened. The next morning, as thoughts came to my mind of the therapist, my body felt sexualized. I was horrified and ashamed of this temptation. My thoughts grew fuzzy causing me to question my salvation. What had started out as a praise journey on Monday ended up in exhausting warfare by mid-week.

I wrestled with my thoughts for days, which led into a month. At times I felt strong and unwavering in my faith, and then fear and confusion swung like a pendulum in my head. The battle was so intense and alluring that I felt a physical pull, as if the gates of hell were sucking me in both legs at a time. I tossed and turned in bed, wondering if I should return to this therapist. Was this a trigger, a temptation, or an attack from the enemy?

My story illustrates how common it is for women who have experienced sexual intrusion to be sexualized and experience sexual temptation. Our emotions and bodies respond instinctively and involuntarily in ways that we cannot control. Many survivors act out sexually as a response to the sexualization they experienced in their abuse. Sexual temptation may come from triggers, but it is important to remember that our experience may be a combination of a trigger, a temptation, and a spiritual attack.

Confession Makes Us Strong

The word tells us to confess our sin to one another and we will be healed (Jam. 5:16). During this time of temptation, I shared with my close friend Carrie, how I felt stable one moment and then pulled down the next. She listened and didn't judge me. I felt relieved. Her mercy allowed me to move ahead with hope. In fact, she affirmed she could see the enemy attacking me. Her loving spirit permitted me to keep my eyes on Jesus. With her gracious response, I felt that if I did fall into temptation, I could go back to her and she would kindly point me back to God. This is what Jesus' grace does for us. When we fear judgment we tend to isolate from others, but God's kindness allows us to honestly admit our struggles (Rom. 2:4).

When you wrestle with hard issues, ask for godly help. Call a friend and ask her for prayer. Connect with someone who will be gracious and speak truth. This connection can keep us safe in times of temptation. Remember Jesus took on our battle and endured suffering. As our High Priest, he understands our trials and temptations. Jesus is mercy-hearted; he's not our judge.

God's Assurance through Creation

God uses circumstances to get our attention. He always uses the word, but God often speaks to me through nature. He may choose something different for you.

During this battle, God brought me comfort through birds. Occasionally in summer, a bright yellow finch will alight on our bird feeder. One morning, not one, not two, but three of my winged friends fed together. Captivated, by these little creatures, I interpreted this winged-holy-huddle as the God-head showing up. Like a cheering squad!

The next day, while doing stretch exercises on my back porch, a bird's melodic tune sounded above me. My eyes spotted his little shape from the branch. His sweet twitter lifted my heavy spirit. Then, as if instructed by God, it hopped down a branch, cocked its head, and sang right to me!

But the battle raged. Each day, multiple triggering thoughts bombarded my mind saying, *you are unworthy, you have failed*. I struggled with my thoughts and turned to the Lord and to his truth about me and felt relief.

A few days later, my heart felt heavy-laden as I pushed my grandkids on their swings. My mind ruminated over my temptation, when a screeching sound came from the woods. A large bird immerged from a tree and soared effortlessly over our heads, with the tips of its feathers dancing in the air. Underneath, its body bore soft white feathers. I like to think that God understood my battle and he sent a bird to hover over me.

When has God encouraged your spirit through his creation?

God's Armor to Strengthen You

The armor of God will protect us in battle. Paul, a fellow sufferer, who spent many days chained in a damp, dark, friendless prison, encourages us to stand against our enemy. He explains our struggle is unseen. We war against invisible evil authorities and spiritual forces even in the heavenly realms. Paul directs us to dress ourselves with protective equipment to stand steady when the day of evil comes. Truth binds us around the waist like a belt. God honors truthful living. Another piece of our spiritual armor is the shield of faith. When we put our faith in Jesus, he distinguishes the flaming arrows of Satan. The helmet and the sword of the Spirit are the Word. A helmet protects us from trouble and the Word keeps us strong. We are instructed to keep on praying, so we can stand and be fearless (Eph. 6:13-18).

I needed to make a decision when it came to my struggle with the medical massage professional. My sexual temptation wanted me to keep seeing him and the voice in my head told me I was making a big deal out of nothing. However, in my mind, I knew I should end my sessions with him. In any battle, we need godly direction, so I asked the Lord for wisdom. Should I go back and confront this man or cut my ties? My people pleasing wanted to avoid confronting him, but I knew I needed to face the truth and let him know his behavior had crossed a line.

That afternoon I was on a ladder staining my grandkid's swing set when I leaned too far and the ladder teetered and folded closed. I tumbled down without breaking any bones. Later, I called and cancelled my future appointments. In addition, I emailed and confronted him about his unprofessional behavior. I felt empowered when he apologized in return.

You may be facing a battle. Put on God's full armor and lean into him.

Keep Singing to Stay Strong

Sometimes in a spiritual battle, praising God can change the dynamics of the struggle. When I was a teenager, not more than thirteen, a missionary from my home church taught me to praise the Lord no matter what. While over for lunch one afternoon she said, "Lynne, if you have a problem, remember whatever it is, just start praising the Lord." Tune your heart to him, and he will bring you above the trouble."

I put singing to practice. In the coat closet next to my office, I stow a large clear bag of instruments (I often pull it out when my grandkids come). It's filled with jingle-bell wristbands, wooden whistles, and various sized tambourines. When I want to acknowledge a client's growth, it's cause for celebration. I say, "Let's shake a tambourine!" Sometimes I say it for effect, but other times I find my yellow tambourine and actually shake it. We laugh, but it gives us great joy. Celebrating is a great way to mark growth.

After the Israelites crossed the Red Sea on dry land, Moses' sister Miriam grabbed a tambourine and danced and sang with the other women. Here is part of her song:

> Sing to the Lord, for he is highly exalted. The horse and its rider he has hurled into the sea. The Lord is my strength and my song; he has become my salvation (Ex. 15:1-3) Your right hand, O Lord, was majestic in power. Your right hand, O Lord, shattered the enemy. In the greatness of your majesty you threw down those who opposed you (Ex. 15:6-7).

Envision that scene. Let it inspire you. What area of your life can you celebrate?

Lynne Head

A Battle Makes Us Stronger

God may use a battle to make us stronger. What might God be preparing you for through testing? After Jesus' temptation, God strengthened him with angels who attended his needs (Matt. 4:11). Jesus understands testing and sympathizes with us when we are tempted. Let's resist Satan's attacks with the help of his Spirit. But remember, if we fail, God is merciful and always ready to forgive us when we cry out to him.

PART FOUR

Freedom to Live

CHAPTER SIXTEEN

Finding Forgiveness

The act of forgiveness necessitates a passage through hell.

Last night I got in a spat at a restaurant with one of my daughters. Since I have a special diet, I skipped the bread, ordered half the meat and doubled the veggies. My daughter, an experienced waitress, explained firmly this would inconvenience the server, as there wasn't a button on the computer to make the change. But I insisted that with my food restrictions, I needed to ask.

In order to resolve our differences, we needed to talk, listen, and respect each other's viewpoint. Once we understood one another, I decided not to ask for changes at corporate restaurants in the future and she affirmed she would empathize more with my food challenges.

Abuse and the Act of Forgiveness

Forgiveness for an abuse survivor doesn't compare to settling differences in a restaurant squabble, yet there is a principle we may take from this example. In order to forgive on a larger scale, we need to view life from God's perspective and understand the life of our offender.

Jesus describes our forgiveness of those who sin against us as something we offer repeatedly...seventy times seven (Matt. 18:22). If we do the math, forgiveness feels impossible. Why would Jesus expect abused people to forgive? How can we forgive our offender's sick and selfish acts? You may feel defensive just thinking about it.

Imagine the act of forgiveness as unlikely as you having the strength and desire to push open a large door overgrown with old vines to reach a hidden garden. Reaching for the door may bring pain, a prick from thorns, a splinter, even a fierce burn. The door may seem heavy and hard to move. But on the other side, beauty could be uncovered and even a pleasant fragrance found where deadness has settled.

Forgiving our offender may never bring us warm feelings towards him. But as we trust Jesus who experienced unjust harm, we too can find comfort and courage.

The Desire for Justice

Have you ever been so full of anger and bitterness, you wanted to kill your offender? I have. Yet taking the life of another would never compensate for the offenses of our abusers. If I murdered my offender for real, or in my mind, it would only increase my hatred and never give me true satisfaction.

Since we are made in God's image, we hold value as humans. This sense of dignity demands that wrong be made right. It is not wrong to desire a rapist be sent to jail. However, as humans we lack the power to bring complete and total retribution for the offenses committed by a sex offender. Only God has the right and ability to pay back vengeance (Heb. 10:30).

Nevertheless, God demands justice as well. His flawless character is holy and nothing unclean can come before him. But God loved us so much that he made a way to satisfy his anger against our sin through the sacrifice of his Son, Jesus (Jn. 3:16).

Isaiah the prophet foretold of Jesus' death:
> Surely he took up our infirmities and carried our sorrows,
> yet we considered him stricken by God,
> smitten by him, and afflicted.
> But he was pierced for our transgressions,
> he was crushed for our iniquities;
> the punishment that brought us peace was upon him,
> and by his wounds we are healed.
> We all, like sheep, have gone astray,
> each of us has turned to his own way;
> and the Lord has laid on him
> the iniquity of us all (Is. 53:4-6).

Jesus took our rage and abuse on himself. His punishment and his wounds heal us.

One year at Easter while living in France, God brought me healing release to forgive Mike by watching Mel Gibson's, *The Passion of the Christ*. Normally, I don't look at the beatings and crucifixion, but this time my eyes fastened on Jesus' face with every lash of the whip, pull of the beard, and hammer of the nail. Each anguished cry Jesus uttered brought a sense of justice to my suffering.

By acknowledging the brutality Jesus took on my offender's behalf, my heart could relinquish its anger. Jesus' blood cleansed the hatred I harbored against him. Now, in trusting Jesus' payment, I chose to forgive. I felt free from anger and could open my heart again.

Knowing the sacrificial love of Jesus will help us forgive the horrific abuse we've taken from the hands of our offenders. If Jesus' payment for sin was sufficient to satisfy God's holy wrath, then should it also not satisfy my own? Jesus asked us to forgive not to make life hard, but to set us free. Releasing our offender from the heart produces healing. How might Jesus' afflictions quiet your heart toward your offender? Practice imagining Jesus saying, "It is finished" when you feel the desire to get revenge (Jn. 19:30).

The Unmerciful Servant

Sexual intrusion is evil and wounding and feels unforgivable. As battle-weary survivors, we mourn over our bodies and the ripple effects of abuse in our relationships. We wonder why God allowed the abuse.

Jesus told a story that helps us gain a better perspective with this battle. A king counted the debt of his servant and decided to sell him, his family, and all his belongings to pay back what he owed. When the servant begged the king to forgive his enormous debt, the king *felt pity and had a change of heart,* and let the servant go (Matt. 18:21-35).

As the servant left, he searched for a fellow owing him a fraction of his debt and demanded his money. Ignoring the servant's pleas, he grabbed him by the neck and threw him in jail.

When the king received word of this, he asked the servant, "How could you do such a thing after I had forgiven you so much? Shouldn't you have had mercy too?" Therefore, the king sent him to jail to be tortured until he could pay back everything (Matt. 18:33-34).

What kept a man who was forgiven such a great debt from being merciful to his fellow man who owed him a small debt? As an abuse survivor, how and why should we show mercy to our offender?

At times, our sin may seem slight compared to the violent abuse done to us. But aren't we just like the king's servant who refused to forgive?

God's Mercy

The unmerciful servant failed to see the king's heart of mercy, therefore he had no ability to show mercy to someone else. Mercy is letting someone go. Though the unmerciful servant saw he had a great debt and begged the king to release him, his heart was unchanged by the king's mercy. His hardness of heart blinded him and consequently, his lack of mercy resulted in a life of misery and torture.

In order for abuse survivors to forgive, we need to see our lives from God's perspective. Like the king who had pity, God has pity on our sin. And though our offender can never pay us back for the abuse he committed against us, God shows us that our sin against him is immeasurably more than our offender's sin against us.

We need forgiveness for the many ways we live without a thought for God. Our hearts must be touched by the enormity of our debt against God. Although we have been victims of horrendous crimes, we too, have been agents of sin. This is a difficult truth for us as abuse survivors to accept. But God is understanding. He is a merciful king who changes his heart from anger to love towards those indebted to him. His kindness came when he let his own Son bear the payment necessary as punishment for our sins (Tit. 3:4-7). How could our hearts not be touched by God's mercy?

Herein lies the path to forgiveness; we must open our hearts to the merciful loving Father, acknowledge our inability to pay for our sins, trust him and receive the free gift of forgiveness through Jesus' death. God's kindness towards our rebellious sin can then lead us to turn from our sin and forgive others (Rom. 2:4). When we admit our sins, he will forgive us—and we become able to forgive. That's worth celebrating!

Ask God for the humility to reflect on your own offenses and bring your heart to God, our loving and merciful Father.

Blindness to Our Sin

What if we have difficulty seeing our own sin? How do we learn to see? God gave Moses the ten commandments to show his people how to live and stay in fellowship with him (Ex. 20:1-17). Although God knew it was impossible to keep the law, he gave the law to help us see our need for him. Rom. 3:19-20 says,

> "Now we know that whatever the law says, it says to those who are under the law, so that every mouth may be silenced and the whole world held accountable to God. Therefore no one will be declared righteous in God's sight by the works of the law; rather, through the law we become conscious of our sin."

The law exposes our sin. We will either open ourselves to admit we are sinners and soften to our need to receive the gift of Jesus' forgiveness, or we will harden ourselves in pride and become blind to our need. When we see our sin, we simply ask God to forgive us.

> But from everlasting to everlasting the Lord's love is with those who
>
> Fear him, and his righteousness with their children's children—
>
> With those who keep his covenant and remember to obey
>
> his precepts (Ps. 103:17-18).

How to Forgive, Count the Debt

In the story of the unmerciful servant, the king counted the debt of the servant before he let it go. Counting the debt is like a victim impact statement in court. It means we name the losses and identify the hurts of the abuse. Forgiveness does not mean we forget. In fact, remembering our abuse will give us discernment in relating to our offenders in the future. Forgiveness could take days, even years—we need time to process our denial, to verbalize and grieve the impact.

Is there an offense that pains you? You may want to make a list of your losses and then take time to grieve them. You could imagine your offender in a chair and talk to them or you could draw a picture of your abuse and walk through your thoughts and feelings. Ask a pastor or friend to pray with you. Be patient. It may take a year or two in counseling to forgive your offender. The process of forgiveness invites us to grieve our wounded heart. You may scream, burst out in curses, or hit the table with your fist. Take time to count the cost. Remember Jesus' bloody sacrifice for you as you remember your own hell. Lean on his wounds to comfort your soul. Jesus went through hell, lived in hell, and rose from hell to save us from ours.

What About My Reservations?

Although it would give tremendous validation to us if our offender acknowledged their wrongdoing, when confronted it is likely our offender will deny, minimize, or not remember what they've done. But we don't need our offender to apologize in order to forgive them.

When Jesus hung on the cross, he had mercy on those who put him to death even though they never apologized and, in some cases, were proud of their actions. In many cases, our offenders have no idea of the bearing their words or actions have on us. Jesus' sufferings and sacrifice allow us to forgive those who are unrepentant.

Jesus instructs us to go to the person who sinned against us (Matt. 18:15-19). This is a matter which takes time and thought. We might need the advice from a counselor on assessing whether our offender is teachable or in an appropriate state of mind. We may need to weigh the pros and cons. But if you do decide to confront your offender, there are options. You could write a letter or make a phone call. You could meet in a public setting for protection. The goal is to share how the abuse hurt you, and what you desire in return from them.

I confronted Mike in the car on my ride home back to school. His initial denial brought fierce anger in my heart. When we said goodbye, he said he was sorry, but I was in no condition to receive his quick apology. He had no idea how his sin had affected me, and neither did I have enough time to grieve over the offense.

If your offender sees their fault and asks forgiveness, that's a gift. However, if your offender does not acknowledge their wrongdoing, you may need to set firm limits in your relationship.

God says he loves justice, and his throne is established on justice (Ps. 9:4). He will end all evil on judgment day (Rev. 20). Knowing this may not bring immediate comfort to our present hardships, but it does give us hope there will be an end to sexual abuse and God will punish all offenders.

Forgiveness on a Personal Note

Forgiveness in my own life has been a process. Just as the king in the parable of the unmerciful servant counted the debt due him, I too had to count the cost.

One day as I felt comfortless from the effects of abuse, God showed me Psalm 62. "My soul finds rest in God alone; my salvation comes from him. He alone is my rock and my salvation; he is my fortress, I will never be shaken" (Ps. 62:1-2). The timing of this gave my heart rest in God's love and strength.

Counting the cost brought conflicting feelings inside me. On our mission trip, Mike and Nan paid attention to us younger adults. We talked and cracked jokes. My heart anguishes over the memory of those good times I shared with them, compared to the hurt they afflicted on me a short time later. Hatred and sadness rise in me to think that Mike planned to use me. I'm angry to think he intentionally groomed me. When I took time to count the cost, I felt like hitting him or at least giving him a good tongue lashing. I felt shame through my body when I thought back upon those unforgettable moments. Abuse cost me. I trusted that Jesus' personal sacrifice by giving himself to physical beatings, and by his willingness to become a victim of abuse, would satisfy the cost abuse brought me. I wanted him to nurse my emotional bruises with comforting touch.

Forgiving Mike and Nan came when I saw life from their perspective. They too, were imperfect like me. They had their own hurts and needs. Mike had money, power, and prestige, but they didn't fulfill him. He needed Jesus.

Nan didn't have the guts to tell Mike to stop. Maybe she complained, but she couldn't stop him. The only answer I have for any abuse survivor is to bring it—the ugly, raw abuse and yourself—to Jesus.

Let your heart be touched today with Jesus' presence. Listen for God's Spirit gently calling your name.

Imperfect Parents

A friend asked, "Are you going to write anything about God the Father?" She expressed disappointment in her earthly father—"If he had watched where I was and what I was doing, maybe the abuse wouldn't have happened."

For many women, disappointment with their earthly father runs deep. Our fathers may have abandoned us, physically or emotionally. Maybe a dad or stepdad, grandfather, or uncle abused you. These devastating feelings of grief and loss may cause us to project the disappointment and hatred of our father feelings onto God. Listen to these words of comfort; they are not my words, but God's words:

> Zephaniah 3:17:
> The Lord your God is with you, he is mighty to save.
> He will take great delight in you, he will quiet you with his love,
> He will rejoice over you with singing.

The truth is, God wept over what happened to you, and over what may still be happening. Psalms 34:18 says, "The Lord is close to the brokenhearted and saves those who are crushed in spirit." One day, if not now, God will hold your father (stepfather, uncle, or grandfather) responsible for his actions. We know that the sexually immoral who have not been pardoned by the blood of Jesus will be thrown in the fiery lake of burning sulfur (Rev. 21:8).

God the Father protects you. Hear the words of David,

> "I will exalt you, O Lord, for you lifted me out of the depths and did not let my enemies (offenders) gloat over me. O Lord my God, I called to you for help and you healed me. O Lord, you brought me

up from the grave; you spared me from going down into the pit" (Ps. 30:1-2).

Abuse feels like we've gone to the grave. A living death. A friend of mine confided in me about her anger towards her father. While in prayer one day, God said to her, "What about your sin?" She found God's mercy for her own sin and consequently forgave her father.

I've also heard heart-wrenching pain from women who struggle to forgive their mothers. These adult women are hurt little girls with moms who were too busy to teach or guide them. Their moms may have been jealous, insecure or looked the other way. You may be one such woman who desperately wanted the love and tenderness of your mother.

How does the heavenly Father's love enable you to process forgiveness for your imperfect parents? I pray Jesus' deep concern and care for you will touch your soul.

What If I Don't Feel I Have Forgiven?

I'd like to share a last thought about forgiveness. Forgiveness is ongoing. We might choose a moment in time to forgive our offender, but painful conflicting feelings may crop up when you get triggered, causing you to question whether you've forgiven your offender. In the midst of the pain, we'll have to choose again and again to let it go. Could this be what Jesus meant by the seventy times seven?

Forgiveness is the result of a changed heart. If your heart is hard and needs softening, come to Jesus. He speaks to God on your behalf. God's mercy will flow from his Spirit over you like a soothing wind. The act of forgiveness will hurt and cost you, but it will unfold beauty and strength from within you. Trust me, when you capture the kindness and love of God, the condition of your heart can turn from hatred to peace.

CHAPTER SEVENTEEN

Transforming Shame

O God, shine on me with Your grace
strengthen me to believe what You say is true
Open my heart and set me free—
to sing out my song to You.

I have this funny habit at night. I moan in my sleep. At least this is what my husband tells me. Sometimes I'm half awake and hear myself groan with regret and embarrassment over something I said in error that day. It's like I'm having a bad dream.

Dealing with Illegitimate Shame

Survivors of unwanted sexual intrusion have a common struggle with shame. Satan loves to hold us in bondage with these feelings like the unconscious sighs I utter while I'm sleeping. Shame produces self-contempt; it's a lie, telling us we are flawed and inferior. These worthless feelings drive us into all kinds of sinful patterns.

Yet, illegitimate shame is not sin as much as it is a distorted belief. It's a skewed perspective of who we are. Shame can be powerful. Recently I have battled with weight gain. I try to live and eat healthy which is way more important than the numbers on the scale. However, I've gained a few of those unwanted pounds, probably due to menopause (ugh) and from medication (double ugh). Anxiety rises in my chest even as I type this. At times, I compare myself to friends and think I need to try harder to exercise or control my eating habits. But transforming shame means I believe God accepts and loves me in spite of my weight, and I know I need to let go of my self-loathing.

Turning away from illegitimate shame means diving down through all those awful feelings of inferiority and submerging deeper into the knowledge that we are quite safe in God's loving arms. As daughters, knowing our acceptance comes from God, we can redirect our focus from panic mode to rest mode. We can be still. "In repentance and rest is your salvation, in quietness and trust is your strength…" (Is. 30:15).

Sexually abused women face a dark valley of shame and fear. Countless women I've listened to describe how their abuse kept them silent for years. One woman explained how she was abused as a child, a teenager, and while pregnant as a young adult. Now, in her fifties, she is breaking out of the silence and bravely working through the fear that stalked her.

What thoughts or experiences bring you shame?

Legitimate Shame

Often our unhealthy responses to illegitimate shame lead us to sin which causes legitimate shame. Legitimate shame is the result of wrongdoing. Our abuse may lead us to respond to life's disappointments with a behavior that has turned into an unhealthy pattern. For instance, one girl who suffered abuse by a family member habitually had to drink, just to relax enough to have sex with her husband. Although her desire to come together with her husband is admirable, it misses a more important reality, her heart. She knew the use of alcohol only covered her pain and hid the real her. The core problem was not the use of alcohol, but that she used it to mask significant parts of her true self, which is what she needed to engage in a healthy relationship. Her hiding kept her relying on herself and living apart from God and her husband.

As God's daughters, we have the freedom to come to him with our raw, naked self. Believing he has blotted our legitimate and illegitimate shame, we then can risk exposing our inner selves because Jesus himself cancelled all of our shame by dying on the cross. Though our sin may feel significant, his mercy for us is far greater. Understanding his mercy allows us to receive him and live as if we are not condemned for our sin. This is the key to transforming our shame.

We have a new identity without the baggage of shame that empowers us to say no to any sin because we are not obligated to our flesh or what feels good but are free to do good. Jesus' death freed us from this pattern to our flesh. Living by God's Spirit enables us to choose his good rather than the misdeeds of our natural desire. Through faith in Jesus and trust in the Spirit's power that raised him from the dead, we free ourselves from the effects of abuse (Rom. 8).

You may think God can't forgive you. Yet, when we have sinful responses to abuse, God's mercy is always available to us. Anytime we cry out, he listens. We rejoice because our sins aren't counted against us.

My friend Amy shared the transforming help she found:

> Acknowledging my brokenness and my own poor and sinful choices, I humbled myself before God. In that moment I knew I could trust him with my wounded heart. He is holy and I am his through Jesus. There was no more shame; joy and peace replaced anger and hurt. My past is the same, but I now see God at work through those painful moments. Praise God, I am no longer living dead!

Remind yourself of the affection Christ has for you. What part of your real self could you make vulnerable to him?

Holding on to Dignity and Desire

One of the ways we know we're beginning to free ourselves from illegitimate shame is by living from our God-given desires. Desires are what we long for or wish for. They are our wants. Understanding our dignity or value in God helps us move into our desires wisely. Without dignity, our behavior toward others would have no bounds and our respect for ourselves would be limited. For our dignity is what allows us to respect ourselves and another human being.

Desire is a tricky thing. We can have over-desire or under-desire. For example, when we live with over-desire, we tend to be greedy and when we live with under-desire we tend to live restrained. Either style of living can become self-focused. But resting in God's love for us and living for him produces godly living.

In Francis Shaeffer's, *True Spirituality*, he describes the potential danger of desire that can lead to greediness and envy, or over-desire. Our desires can become idolatrous by putting something above God. When we don't get what we want, our desire can lead to discontentment and ingratitude.

Over-desire tends to sport a lifestyle of indulgence, which can also be an escape for one who has experienced sexual abuse. Over-desire can drive someone into a life of partying and easy sex. An abuse survivor that lives an indulgent wild side of life needs to rest her desires in God's love and forgiveness. Only then, can she make good boundaries and have self-control in decisions and relationships.

If we live with illegitimate shame, we tend to under-desire. We don't own up to our desire, we downplay it. Transforming shame means giving ourselves permission to rise above our shame by resting in God's love and the dignity in which he made us. For a survivor of sexual abuse, this could mean allowing yourself to date, dress without the fear of being lovely, or being more open and trusting in relationships.

At times it's tempting and easier to live in extremes or opposites, with all or nothing, or black and white thinking. Often dysfunctional homes are either more chaotic or very controlled. But living in the tension of under or over desire forces us to take a look at ourselves and our motives. Underneath our actions are our unseen beliefs. Believing in our dignity under God's design gives us rest. We don't have to over work and we're not satisfied with working under our potential either. Most importantly, trusting God with our desires and living for him results in a better outcome than if we rely on ourselves.

I tend to live with under-desire. I have to move out and speak up. When I turn from my shame, and believe that I am a loved daughter, desire increases in my heart. I feel a new freedom for example, to enjoy the world around me like material things. Transforming shame means refusing to loathe myself and trusting God's love and my dignity. Maybe you can identify. In the past, when I spent money on myself, worthless feelings overwhelmed me. This was illegitimate shame.

Repentance, or turning, allowed me to move through my shame and plunge deeper into God's love for me. Knowing God loved me gave me the freedom to enjoy shopping more, like buying jewelry.

One day I went into one of my favorite stores and found a green beaded bracelet. As I handed my card to the salesclerk, I thanked God for the confidence to make this purchase. I enjoyed wearing this small treat and gradually the grace of turning from shame brought new life to me. To live in my desire felt scary, but staying in it allowed me to settle into the gift of God's love.

Turning from shame also allowed me to stop skimping on myself. For instance, I had this weird thought that if I used lotion on my body, I would waste it. I believed the lie that I wasn't worth a little luxury. This meant believing the truth. Living like a daughter of worth meant I allowed myself to have an adequate amount. Now, I permit myself a normal portion. This followed in other areas. I allowed myself an afternoon snack or gave myself another portion at a meal. My body relaxed. I stopped trying to control so many things motivated by the thought that I didn't deserve anything. I was becoming free!

Breaking from shame meant I learned not to hurry. When I lived in France, when leaving the grocery,[1] I used to run to my car with my cart! I wasn't in a rush to get home, I just couldn't slow down. I believed I had to work hard. Enjoying life was not an option. What a lie and deception of the enemy! Believing I was God's loved daughter permitted me to slow down and purposefully enjoy myself. I thanked God for the Robin's eggshell blue sky. I filled my lungs with fresh air and walked deliberately with the heels of my feet on the ground.

What areas in your daily life do you tend to over-desire or under-desire? How would knowing your dignity allow you to rest in God's forgiveness and love and change your desires to make healthier choices?

God's Love Gave Me a Voice

As I turned from shame to resting in my dignity and God's love, I learned to lean into his strength and express my opinions.

Although it terrified me, I also learned to have a voice defending my children. As I was writing this, my son Andrew had been unjustly treated by a teacher. He was fifteen and I was forty-five at the time. Acknowledging my weakness, I prayed, "God give me strength to open my mouth and speak." I went to the school and God gave me the power to speak to the principle. When they ignored my request to speak to the teacher, I wrote a letter and complained and also stated I forgave their misjudgment of him. I never heard back from them, but I felt empowered for following through to protect him. It was important for me to protect my children, especially because in the past, I didn't have the voice to do so for myself.

A huge fruit of this transition from shame came in the area of asking for help. I used to avoid asking for meals from church after a surgery, for a friend to watch my kids, or for help packingwhen I moved. I recognized how independent and scared I felt. I thought so little of myself, I couldn't imagine anyone wanting to assist me. Reminding myself I have dignity, helped me speak up.

How easy is it to use your voice when you need help, or to stand up for your family members? This may be an area of growth for many of us.

Learning to Receive

How can receiving be an evidence of change or transforming shame? Last week, I went shopping at some outlets with my hubby and I bought a pair of jeans, a sweatshirt, and a sweater. At church the next day, I obsessed about what I was wearing and compared myself to every woman within a twenty-foot radius. Did I have the right shoes and jeans? Did I have the right hair style? It drove me crazy! I was there to worship, but instead I felt insecure and distracted.

The sermon reminded us about God's desire to bless Abraham. The pastor however, gently warned us not to get caught up in our culture of material things and success. Of course, my mind was panged with guilt about my shopping, so in efforts to control and tame the good desire I had, I beat myself up and decided I could take a sweater back and use my Christmas money to pay for my stuff.

As I was singing the last song, "The Lord bless you and let his face shine on You," I was reminded of God's desire to bless me. I imagined an angel with white wings extending over me. Her beauty calmed my troubled thoughts. On the way home, I shared my struggle with Jim, who agreed that I needed the clothes I bought. (He's always willing for me to buy the clothes I guilt myself for buying). Without shaming myself, I received the clothes as gifts from Jim and the Lord.

Opening my heart to receive from God and from others gave me permission to let go of my shame. Shame kept me from believing I had a sense of dignity in the eyes of God. I chose to believe God wanted to give to me.

How well do you let yourself enjoy receiving? Believe in your worth and identity as a daughter.

Engaging With Men Without Shame

As I grew in my freedom from illegitimate shame, my relationships have improved with men. By believing I'm loved and I have a voice, I can sit next to a man more calmly. Forgetting my former avoidance, I offer words of encouragement to men in my small group at church. God's given me grace talking on the phone with men and even counseling men. I have confronted men when I needed a boundary to keep me safe. What a great relief this has been to me—to speak.

These inner changes have resulted in deeper intimacy with my husband. I have grown in sharing my heart and my needs with him. Living out of my desire rather than shutting it down has been all together new and life giving.

I have shared some of my newfound ways of relating with other women. It is often encouraging to see I'm not alone.

Janice, a friend of mine, shared her transformation:

> I remember the very day, the very place when I was able to look into a man's eyes and see his smile and be okay. What a day that was because prior I could not look into the eyes of a man without feeling like he wanted to have sex with me. Just making eye contact would send that feeling right through my body.
>
> But this day was different, it was redemptive! I was in Yellowstone National Park, walking down the staircase going towards Old Faithful. I became aware of an approaching man and our eyes caught each other. Instead of turning away, dropping my head and feeling the awful fear inside, there was a smile, a sparkle in his eye, and an exchange of hellos.
>
> What an unbelievable moment this was for me; a shift, something new was beginning in me. I could actually look into the eyes of a man and just see him, and he saw me. It was an experience, that moment of beauty. Such freedom!

How would living out of your new identity make a difference? In what relationship do you need to assert yourself or be willing to receive?

As I experienced growth in my life I saw changes that not only came to my personal life, but to other relationships as well. In my counseling practice, although I don't always share the story of my abuse, there are frequent times where I pass on principles of what I learned to others.

Breaking through shame becomes redemptive when we see God use our stories. Listen to the story of Helena, who broke through her shame and spoke about her abuse:

> While living overseas, for the first time I felt safe from my perpetrators and started counseling.

Months later in 2014, I was asked to share about healing from my childhood sexual abuse with a group of girls at a Christian school.

Seven years later in 2021, my teen-age daughter bounced home from school, talking about a terrific guest speaker (an alumni of the school). The speaker shared how God helped her resist sexual temptations in college and encouraged the girls to trust God and remain sexually pure.

A few days later, Mrs. Chase, the teacher of the class, told me this speaker was one of the young girls I spoke to seven years earlier! I was elated to see God pass fruit from my life to this young woman to my daughter.

We learn that transformation in our life can mean transformation in the lives of our children. And that is worth celebrating.

Transforming shame is like taking a bag of old clothes to Good Will and buying yourself a new wardrobe at your favorite shop. Only this transformation takes place on the inside and our new inner self doesn't fade with age. When God covers our shame, he holds us steady, we experience a stillness and solitude that brings comfort and peace. He takes us from shame to a deeper closeness.

CHAPTER EIGHTEEN

Developing Closeness

It matters to You when I cry
Jesus, take my face in Your hands
touch my cheeks with Your fingers,
look me in the eyes.

Before my husband pursued me as his serious girlfriend, we had a discussion. He had lots of female friends, yet I didn't feel secure in our relationship until he made a commitment to single me out from the others. We can have this same assurance in a relationship with Jesus. At times, Jesus may feel as distant as the clouds in the sky, but when we experience him in a personal way, the intimacy we share with Jesus can surpass any love we have ever felt on earth.

Jesus offers us a love not unlike the love between a man and woman. After all, we are the bride of Christ. Scripture identifies the love between a married man and woman as a covenant before God. The beautiful reality is that God offers a believer this same covenant relationship with himself, no matter what one's marital status.

A relationship with Jesus reveals the blessing and beauty of intimacy. When two people love each other they develop an inner circle with a shared bond. When we enter into a relationship with Jesus, we enter into his union with God the Father and God's Spirit. The three share an intimate union working together.

When we value someone important to us, we make spending time with them a priority. For instance, if you have surgery or give birth to a baby, you choose people that mean the most to you to provide the comfort and support you need. Spending time together produces cherished memories.

Another way we indicate our closeness to those we love is how we say goodbye. When Jim and I moved to France, there were many rounds of goodbyes including churches, neighbors, friends, and family. Each goodbye became more intimate, from a wider circle of friends to closer friends, then to family.

Jesus had a need to connect with loved ones. He took time to say goodbye with a close friend, Mary Magdalene, after his resurrection (Jn. 20:10-18). Imagine what Jesus may have thought:

> *I've just paid for the whole worlds' sins and know the agony of separation from my Father. I know how Mary feels, sad and worried about me since my death, so before I return to the Father, I'll reassure her I'm alive and that everything's going to be okay.*

What a beautiful moment for Mary Magdalene when Jesus came to her. Jesus wants to spend sweet times like this with us too.

Close Friends Have Special Names

When two people spend a lot of time together, they often assign a special name to each other. A shared name indicates closeness. Jesus wants a special closeness with us and will give each of us a name in heaven, signifying our intimate relationship with him.

Jesus will give us a white stone with a name written on it only known to you and him (Rev. 2:17). The name suggests a change in us. Without the work of Jesus, we couldn't have this new name. This name signifies the truth of who we are, canceling the lies with which the enemy seeks to destroy us.

God changed the name of Sarai to Sarah. She was barren and hopeless, but God meant her to become the mother of nations. God changed Sarah's life from fruitlessness to a life where she flourished and multiplied. God is in the process of changing us and he is using his love relationship to fulfill and satisfy our longings.

Jesus' love transformed my thinking of myself. One afternoon lying on my bed, weeping, feeling worthless and ashamed, I turned to Revelation. My eyes fell on these verses: "for you created all things, and by your will they were created and have their being" (Rev. 4:11b). The Holy Spirit comforted me in an indescribable way. The thought that Jesus fashioned me just the way he wanted gave me confidence that he knew what he was doing. There was no mistake in his creation of me. These words gave me life.

Let the message that God created you sink into your heart. How does this encourage you?

Close Friends Give Gifts

Just as close friends spend time with each other and call each other special names, close friends give gifts. When we think of gift giving, we often think of gifts given for special occasions like birthdays.

When you buy a gift for someone you love, you put special thought into their uniqueness, keeping in mind their likes and dislikes. A gift giver anticipates the surprise and delight of the person receiving the gift.

Another aspect of gift giving produces communication. I smile when my five-year old granddaughter picks me a tiny blue flower and presses it into my hand. In turn, I put my nose to it and shout with exclamations of its beauty. I feel her love and I receive it in love. There is a warm connection in our interaction.

Jesus gives us gifts expressing his intimacy with us. God has given me many such gifts. Some are material and others are personal in nature.

One morning when I was writing about my abuse, I felt down and dirty. My restless heart needed peace. Carrying this heavy spirit into the grocery, I maneuvered between customers and parked my cart by the milk section, when I heard someone wheel up and position his cart in front of me. I looked up to a man with gray hair and wire-framed glasses wearing a plaid flannel shirt. His gentle face put me at ease as his hands rested on the handle of his cart. Our eyes met. He spoke, "Can I tell you something? You're beautiful."

His words entered me like the fragrance of a field of golden daffodils in spring. "Thank you." I felt genuine happiness. And with an unadulterated heart, I felt unafraid. His message ignited me with joy as if wings lifted me off the ground.

I turned my head and he was gone. *Strange.* The man's presence felt other-worldly. God had sent an angel and kissed me with the kindest of words. When we feel God's extraordinary touch in our lives, he draws us closer to himself, filling us with an intimacy better than anything earth has to offer.

CHAPTER NINETEEN

Longing for A Safe Place

If I were in heaven
I would see the Lord's beauty and love,
I would fall upon my face and sing
To the One who reigns above.

Many winters ago, an ice storm covered the town where I lived. The routine and dreary forty-five minute bus ride to school turned cheerful and gave me time to relish the view. From blade of grass to tree branch, every living thing sagged under the weight of frozen rain. Even fences, parked cars, signs, and sidewalks throbbed, solid and stiff. Then the most glorious thing happened. A bright ray of sun peered from behind the trunk of a tree, illuminating the landscape like crystal glass. Sunlight dazzled through every object and my heart felt light with wonder.

Creation Groans and So Do We

Though fallen, creation shouts the glories of life. Creation's beauty kindles power to fill and fixate us, yet it silently groans. Romans 8 describes the wretched dilemma of living in our beautiful but fallen world. Creation groans as a woman in the pains of childbirth waiting to be freed from bondage. We, as fallen but redeemed creatures, groan inwardly, waiting for God to take us from our human existence of suffering to where we'll be free from suffering.

Abuse survivors can feel some of the heaviest, most painful suffering a human being can endure.

In his book, *The Problem of Pain*, C.S. Lewis describes pain as a tool where God speaks loudly to us. Lewis says, "God whispers to us in our pleasures, speaks in our conscience, but shouts in our pain."

This shouting in pain makes us long for another world. Our suffering as abuse survivors causes us to groan and hope for the redemption of our bodies. As we groan, the Spirit of God groans within us searching our hearts and minds. As the Holy Spirit feels our pain and weakness, he cries to God with words that we ourselves cannot express (Rom. 8: 26-27). Life this side of heaven is lived with a longing for something better, a beauty that is only found in heaven.

Heaven, A Place of Hope

Part of managing our suffering here is envisioning a life that will be free of pain and death. This stirs our heart with hope.

> God gives us hope in our suffering. And hope does not disappoint us, because God has poured out his love into our hearts by the Holy Spirit (Rom. 5: 5-6).

Even as we suffer and waste away, our inner spirit is being renewed with hope. What we experience here on earth, though heavy, is from heaven's perspective, light and momentary compared to the beautiful glory that is being produced through our pain. We are encouraged to keep our eyes on the things that are unseen, for what is unseen is eternal (2 Corinthians 4:16-18).

Jesus said that he was going to prepare a place for us and will come back to take us to be with him. He reassured the disciples this was true (John 4:1-4). Heaven will be a place where God will wipe away our tears. There will be no more death, or mourning, or crying or pain (Rev. 21:4).

A Place I'm Known

In *Imagine Heaven,* John Burk describes heaven like a home where you feel welcome. His recounting of Crystal's story of abuse caught my attention. As a young girl from three to eleven, she was sexually abused by babysitters. On one occasion, during a party, one of her mother's boyfriends shot at her, barely missing. She never told her mother about the abuse and trauma and lived in brokenness. Crystal admits she turned far from God, "I saw the hardships in my life as evidence that God had no interest in protecting me from harm." (Burke, 2015, p.68)

Until she died. When Crystal was thirty-three, she went to the hospital for pancreatitis and due to complications, she died for a nine-minute span and went to heaven. This is what she said:

> I was very aware of the fact that I had just died. But I also was the me that had existed from the moment that God had created me. Unlike on earth, where I was plagued by doubts and fears, in heaven there was nothing but absolute certainty about who I was."

She felt all the abuse from her past had evaporated and she knew herself for the first time and had confidence in God's truth about her: "Before I formed you in the womb, I knew you" (Jer. 1:5). (Burke, 2015, p.69)

Crystal tasted life for a moment without suffering from the effects of her abuse. Her temporary experience filled her remaining days on earth with hope for her eternal home. As much as this was comforting, we don't need an experience like Crystal's to feel known and loved this side of heaven. God has powerfully demonstrated his love for us in Jesus here and now, and through the Holy Spirit, we can know and experience God's love and comfort even before heaven.

The Apostle Paul reminds us that on earth we see things unclearly, as looking into an aged mirror, but in heaven our understanding will be crystal clear and we will be fully known (1 Cor. 13:12).

A Place of Beauty

The most vivid descriptions of heaven are found in Revelation chapters four and five and in chapters twenty-one and twenty-two. I often meditate on them to regain a sense of perspective when life here feels despairing. The apostle John sees God sitting on a throne dazzling like a diamond in a crimson sunset. A rainbow of velvet emerald surrounds his throne. God's beauty is described in Psalm 90:17, "May the beauty of the Lord our God be upon us and establish the work of our hands for us; Yes, establish the work of our hands."

In heaven, our pain will turn to praise. This morning I woke early and went out on my front porch where I was greeted by a rose hue breaking the morning sky. Across the street two birds perched, one on each rooftop, joyously singing their tunes. Just think, when Jesus returns with the bright tone of a trumpet call, these momentary touches of heaven on earth will become endless praise.

Our souls will find rest and healing in God's beauty.

A Place of Peace

Heaven is a place of eternal peace. The gates surrounding heaven will never be shut—there will be no need to lock a door, for no one impure will enter (Rev. 21:25-27). Consider what rest might come to your soul, to your mind, to your body, knowing that all abuse will be over. No more dread of someone coming into your home or of anyone threatening to harm you. You won't fear darkness either, for there will be no more night. Instead, the Lord will be our light (Rev. 21:5).

In heaven, we will see God's face (Rev. 22:4). No sin or abuse committed against us will block the light of his love. Come, Lord Jesus.

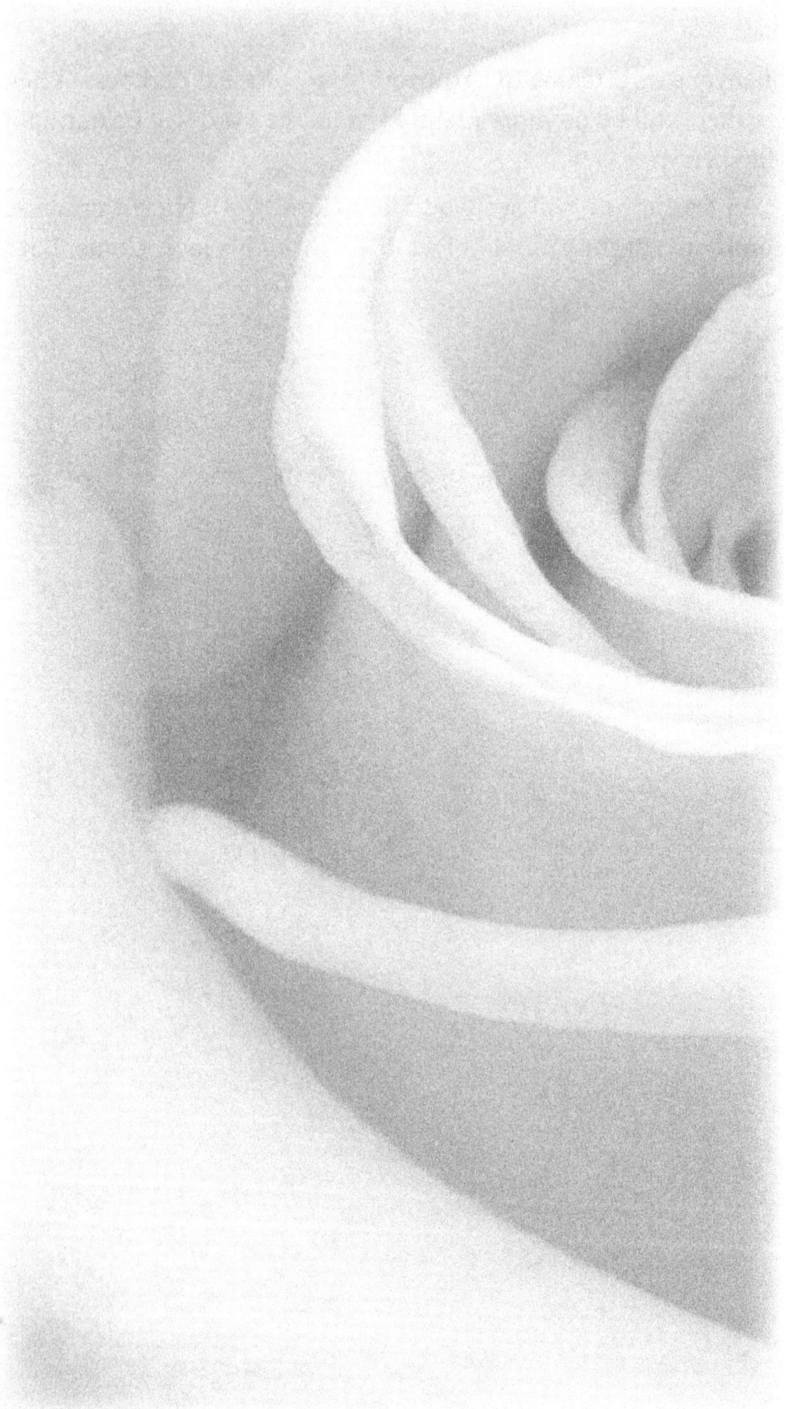

Acknowledgements

To my beautiful Lord who has taken me through many trials to finish this book. When God called me to write my story, I wanted to obey, but I didn't know how to do what seemed beyond my ability. My fear required faith. I started with a willing heart. God gave me grace to go to school and get my license, grace to grieve deep and wide the passing of my precious son, Andrew, and grace to endure such painful and persistent illnesses. But God was faithful, and through my weaknesses of ADD, procrastination, perfectionism, and brain fog, he brought forth people to come alongside me to encourage, pray, and lend their skills. Many times I wondered over eighteen long years whether I would see the end in sight, and again God's grace gave me the faith to believe. God has given me abundantly beyond all I could ask or imagine. I offer this gift of my heart back to God as a reflection of the joy he's brought me.

I thank everyone who joined me to finish the task the Lord set before me. I am grateful for the host of people who prayed for me. Each of you used your specific gifts. Thank you from the wellspring of my heart.

Julie Ann Bakker of Peppertree Publishing. Your vision, energy, and fast-track pacing delivered this dream. Elizabeth Parry, your skills and sensitivity to my ideas in the layout, brought this book together so beautifully.

Candy Abbott, in honor of her vision of Fruitbearer Publishing. Elizabeth Boerner who affirmed me from the first phone call. I know God connected us.

Thank you to Barb Lee, Helen Byrd, and Kathy Clarke for your input and help reviewing my manuscript.

Lauren Craft, my first editor for your gentle spirit, patient instruction, and hours of dedication.

Michele Chynoweth, my final editor for your clear, direct instruction. You asked tough questions that drew my heart to the surface.

To all the women who shared their stories. Your vulnerability and growth reveal God's beauty. Keep your daughter identity strong.

Thank you to many friends who prayed for me including my Email Prayer Ladies, Monday World Team Prayer Ladies, my small groups and pastoral staffs from Southbrook in Weddington and Hope Community in Charlotte. We prayed this through.

Thanks to Jeannie Hartsfield and Susan Best and World Team USA, for your support and coordination in this project.

Special thanks to: Katie Kuepfer, Gabriela Gibson, Konnie Hall, Theresa Bowen, Carrie Miesel, Laura Sommons, Paula Quigley, Jessie Seneca, and Arlene Brokaw. Where would I be without you?

Brandie Muncaster whose spirit causes my heart to leap and makes me want to hear God. Thanks for all your help.

Pete Bondy, whose wisdom helped me discover my desire.

Duane Moyer, for the example of your writing and efforts of encouragement.

Larry Burd, your book came in the mail which encouraged me to continue writing, the same day I asked God whether I should keep going.

Steve Miller, who invested an immeasurable gift of time and valuable coaching skills. This book wouldn't be in peoples' hands without your commitment to helping me finish.

Don Chambers, whose kindness, generosity, and vision has enabled this message to reach across multiple time zones.

Thanks to Jerry Jenkins Writer's Guild, Hope Writers, Christian Writer's Conferences in Spartanburg and Asheville (Les Stobbe, Candy Arrington, Linda Gilden, and Katy Kauffman), for your commitment to inspire and teach the craft of writing.

My parents, who love me and taught me to put Jesus first. I'm grateful for my Straton Christian heritage. To all my siblings and their families and Jim's family for your love, care and prayers for me.

My daughters, Katherine and Laura, whom I love and cherish close to my heart. Thanks for inspiring me. You bring joy to my heart and I am so proud of you.

To my husband, Jim. Thank you for living with me and loving me. I know you are definitely glad this is over. Thank you for your loving labor, cover design, hours of editing, and thoughtful organization you provided into these pages. The timing was perfect. Love you always.

To the Lord for going before me, guiding me, and for what he will yet do.

Appendix 1

Tools of Expression and Communication

Unless you are willing to grieve, you won't find healing. Healthy grief is giving yourself permission to express or explain your thoughts and feelings. I think two of the best ways to express oneself are journaling and art therapy.

Journaling

Journaling is more than verbal expression. Some people like to see what they are thinking and feeling on paper. I totally get this. I can't not write. When I see my thoughts written in ink it's like all this energy has poured out of my body and brain. Writing heals me. If you are the kind of person who likes to write down catchy phrases or take notes during a sermon, you probably like journaling. Buy a journal. It doesn't have to be expensive, a spiral notebook works.

Make a space that feels comfortable and private. I like my back porch in the mornings where birds nest in the trees and scoot out to feed. Other times I go to my office where I get lost in the white noise of the fan. Know yourself. Find a place and make time for you.

Allow adequate time for your level of grief. If you need an hour or more, go for it. If you can only handle thirty to forty-five minutes, go for that. The important thing is to find a safe, quiet place and begin.

Art Therapy

In *Journey to Heal,* Crystal Sutherland discusses how art therapy can be used as a tool of expression and grief. I will list a couple of her suggestions.

> 1) A self-portrait. Draw a self-portrait using pencil, markers, paint or collage expressing how you see yourself. The goal is to express how you see yourself now and choose one thing you want to change. If appropriate share with a trusted friend.
>
> 2) A truth portrait - based on 2 Cor. 5:17, Draw or paint a simple background, on a canvas or piece of paper, like a scene in the country or beach. Next, draw a cross. On the cross, write names you were called, or messages or lies that you experienced. These words will be "nailed" to the Cross with Christ. Then with a different color of pen or paint, write a truth from scripture over these lies that states who you are in Christ. For example, 'I am a slut' is crossed out and in its place I have 'as a bride adorns herself with her jewels' (Is. 61:10).

Here's another suggestion for art therapy, one of my favorites.

> 3) Snap shots of an incident. Draw an experience using four to six simple pictures displaying what happened in each scene. Take a piece of paper and draw a horizontal line across the page, then two vertical lines to make six equal spaces. Start at the beginning of the event and progress through the experience with simple figures. Then describe your thoughts and feelings. Consider the lies or messages. What longings did you experience? What is God's truth about you as a daughter?

Although these exercises can be done in private, these are most powerful when done in community with a trusted friend, counselor, or confidential small group.

Identifying Feeling

Most of us need help finding the right word to express a feeling. Instead of saying, "I feel bad," we can say; "I feel sad and angry. I felt disrespected, shamed, belittled." Finding the right word helps you connect to the inner part of your heart. And can help the person listening to you understand and validate how you feel. You can google and download an assortment of feeling charts.

Naming Our Intensity Level

I'm sure you've been asked by a doctor or nurse, "what is your pain level between one and ten?" It is also useful when we describe a feeling like anxiety. Today, I feel anxious, like an eight. Yesterday, I felt calm like a three or four.

You may prefer words over numbers. For instance, a little bit, medium, high, or overwhelming. My anxiety is medium today, but yesterday it felt overwhelming.

Use this as a guide:

A little bit	Medium	High	Overwhelming

Be creative. You can use your own words or numbers. I have had women tell me, "Today I feel panicky and it's a fifteen!"

Truth Cards

Get a stack of index cards and on one side write a lie you believe. On the back side write what's true about you. Find a verse from scripture and write it underneath the truth. If you like, punch a hole in the upper left or right hand corner and place a metal ring around it to keep them connected. (You can buy these rings at your local store). They serve as a great reminder to get you back on track, especially after a trigger.

Tools of Relaxation

Locate where your body holds stress. Take a mental scan of your body. Do you hold your stress in your chest, hands, head, shoulders, stomach? Draw a stick picture and draw an 'X' on the spot where you feel distress or pain. What is an associated sound? The next time you feel this pain, identify why you are feeling tense. What happened an hour ago or earlier that day? Name three feeling words to describe your emotions.

Breathing

A great breathing exercise is what I affectionately call the nostril. First, take your right thumb and gently close off your right nostril; at the same time breathe slowly up through the left open nostril. Then, with your middle finger, close the left nostril, let go of your thumb on your right nostril and exhale through the right nostril. Now, with your left nostril closed, breath up through the right nostril. Quickly, close your right nostril with your thumb, remove your middle finger from your left nostril and exhale through your left nostril. Repeat 5 times. (I hope you enjoy it as much as I do).

Muscle relaxation

Tense your whole body. Hold your squeeze for five seconds, then let go.

Muscle group relaxation: Start with your shoulders. Tense and hold for five to ten seconds, let go. Work down to your back, tense and hold for five to ten seconds. Now tense and hold your hips and thighs. Now tense your calves, knees, and feet. Let go.

Guided Imagery

Think of your favorite relaxing vacation spot. Do you like the beach or the mountains? Pretend you are at the beach using all five of your senses. Feel sand sliding between your toes and wind tussling your hair, warm sunlight soaking into your skin. Imagine waves crash onshore and lapse offshore. Let the lingering scent from your coconut sunscreen, salt air, and smell of seaweed washed up on shore lift your heavy spirit. Imagine diamonds dancing in circles on blue marine waves. Think of your favorite beach snacks and imagine seagulls snagging your chips. Hear their thankful cries ha-ha-ha-ha.

Music

Find a medium you like. Let it relax your body from stress. Music has powerful effects on your brain.

Tools of Communication

Proverbs tells us that a word aptly spoken is like apples in a bowl of gold. Words bring life or death. Our hearts rise with a genuine compliment and deflate at gossipy or malicious words. Therefore, it's important to practice skills in order to effectively communicate.

Assertiveness

Assertiveness is communicating what you need or want. The problem with our lack of assertiveness is two-fold. We are either consumed by the pressure of pleasing someone or we don't know what our needs and wants are. It takes time reflecting on our physical, emotional, and spiritual needs.

An example of assertiveness: "Honey, I'm worn out watching the kids today. Could you give the kids a bath while I take a walk? I would feel more refreshed to spend together later."

Another example: "Honey, when you look at your phone when I'm talking to you, I feel unimportant. When you look at my face and listen to me, I feel valued and loved." Make sure you tell what difference it would make to you if your request is met.

Active Listening

Assertiveness is essential in good communication, but so is being a good listener. Active listening is not just hearing words, but letting a person know you understand.

An example of active listening: "I hear you saying you want to spend more time with me, but your work is extra busy this week."

Another example: "I hear you saying you feel down about not having friends. You're lonely and depressed."

"I" Statements

"I" statements are effective, less attacking, and can't be judged. Consider the contrast between these two sentences: "You are always so mean to me, I just want to leave." More effective: "I am feeling sad and anxious when you talk to me like that. I am tempted to shut down or leave the house."

More I statements: "I notice you work a lot, but I want to spend time together."

"I feel tense and angry when this job you promised to finish isn't completed."

How to Enter a Conflict (The Four F's)

We don't like conflicts. Sometimes we don't know how to appropriately express disappointment and communicate what we really want or need. Here's another life-changing statement my professor Kevin Huggins said, "The absence of conflict is not the sign of a healthy relationship. All relationships have conflict. A healthy relationship is when two people learn how to solve their problems."

Here's an example of how to enter a potential conflict or a problem that needs solving. I call it the Four F's. Notice we state the facts, then our feelings, and then (for another 'f' sound) what we prefer or affirm. And the final 'f' sound is for the word difference. What difference would it make?

You can practice before you have a conversation. Honey, I noticed when we discussed where to go for dinner yesterday, you spoke to me with that mean tone in your voice (facts); I feel hurt and unloved when you talk to me like that (feelings), and I would like (prefer) if you spoke in a more gentle voice. Maybe we could discuss each other's opinions on restaurant choices. If we did, I would feel more respected and appreciated (difference) and I would better understand your preferences as well.

Here are some other examples:

Step One: State the facts. When you said….or last Saturday night when….or yesterday when xyz happened…

Step Two: Calmly state the emotions and their level of intensity. I felt little a irritated (or I felt intensely hurt and unloved) when you spoke like that.

Step Three: State what you prefer or affirm what you want more or less of. I would like you to be more attentive when I'm talking. Please put your phone down. I would like you to work less and make family time more of a priority.

Step Four: Say what difference, (the f sound) it would make. Don't forget this vital step. If you keep your voice down when we discuss things like where we're going to eat, I would feel loved, important, connected, and be excited to go out on a date with you.

This exercise in communication takes time and practice. Reflect on each step and practice it out loud. It will make a huge difference in problem solving and preventing potential conflicts. Obviously, some conflicts are unavoidable, but when they occur, a good practice after a conflict is to take time to pinpoint where the communication went off course.

Go back to your spouse or friend and rework "I" statements. State the facts, feelings, what you prefer or affirm and how their change in behavior will make a difference. Be an active listener. Problem solve. The next time conflict starts to fester, you'll be more aware of the interchanges taking place and learn how to ameliorate your style of communication.

Taking A Time Out

At times, we all get impatient, angry, and well, downright ugly with our words with our significant other. When our voices rise, we need to de-escalate to keep things from getting out of control. Resist proving your point. Take a time out. Tell the person you are taking a break and will return when you both can talk and actively listen calmly with respect for each other.

Appendix 2

National Sexual Assault Hotline: Available 24 hours. 1-800-656-4673

National Suicide Prevention Hotline: 1-800-273-8255 www.suicidepreventionlifeline.org

National Domestic Violence Hotline 1-800-799-SAFE (7233)

National Human Trafficking Hotline 1-888-373-7888

Substance Abuse and Mental Health Services Administration (SAMHSA) 1-800-662-HELP (4357).

Recommended Reading:

Dan Allender *The Wounded Heart: Hope for Adult Victims of Childhood Sexual Abuse*

Diane Mandt Langberg *On the Threshold of Hope: Opening the Door to Healing for Survivors of Sexual Abuse Suffering and the Heart of God: How Trauma Destroys and Christ Restores*

Mary DeMuth *Not Marked: Finding Hope and Healing after Sexual Abuse*

Paula Rinehart *Sex and the Soul of a Woman*

Crystal M. Sutherland *Journey to Heal: Seven Essential Steps of Recovery for Survivors of Childhood Sexual Abuse*

Bessel van der Kolk *The Body Keeps the Score: Brain, Mind, and Body in the Healing of Trauma*

Aundi Kolber *Try Softer*

Poems

CHAPTER 1 Ride Home

No Longer Victim

Lynne Head

The power of man
tugged at my heart,
numbing fear
paralyzing shame.

Trust broken
shame chosen
worthlessness
grew in my soul.

But now, I know
One greater
who gives life
and strength.

He is bold and tender
safe and gentle,
triumphant
over every wrong.

No longer destined
to walk in danger
voiceless, angry
betrayed, deceived.

No longer victim
to fears I lived
no obligation
to surrender.

My hope, my light
Giver of worth,
no longer victim
with Jesus.

CHAPTER 2 Why Is It So Hard To Talk About?

Reflection

Lynne Head

There are times when
I see my reflection,
I hate what I long
to believe.

There's an image
of me I want to like,
but one I fast
reject.

If truth were said
I long to believe
what is outside
and inside are good.

Believing He put
the mark of His hand
inside and out
of my being.

I long to let
Jesus place
His acceptance
deep within my soul.

From my head to my heart
from my heart to my head,
I want to believe
in His love.

A reflection of Him
a reflection in me,
that's when
I will believe.

Fear, fear, fear in me
fear inside my head.
fear, fear, fear in me
fear inside my heart.

Casting my fear
at His feet
He can restore
His reflection in me.

Jewelry Box

Lynne Head

jewelry box
hides a girl's treasure
keeps safe
valued possessions

there she places
her heart
for fear
of losing it

or betrayal
destroy.
Don't
lift the lid.

Who will restore
security,
courage,
beauty?

The One who created
this little girl,
whose dignity
no one can take.

Open the lid
take out
your
heart

and place
it
within
you

let
His love
pulsate
peace

casting out
all
your
fear.

CHAPTER 3 Why Grieve Over Abuse?

Battle of the Storm

Lynne Head

Terrified
by the storm
turning within
I ignore my fear.

I fight
like a child in a battle—
it is bigger
than I can handle.

Admit I'm
not a warrior,
death lingers.
I let go of my sword.

Feel the terror
I try to scream.
Driving wind and rain,
I can't fight.

Yet in the eye of the storm
rests a quiet, inner place.
I thrust out my hand
I'm feeble but strong.

The storm shakes
and chokes me
such a lonely place-
wavering in a storm.

But You gave me a promise-
You are with me.
I repent of my
control and turn to You.

Help me, God, in this battle of the storm.
Let me find my shelter in You.

A Look Inside

Amy H.

I learned to cope; I moved on;
I regained control; I ...
wore a mask,
and restricted feelings, and limited trust,
and protected my heart so no one could ever betray me again.

And my safe place is no more; was I ever really safe?
Will I ever be?

God is my refuge...
> You didn't protect me; You didn't make it right; You didn't help; You didn't answer, but You saw, and allowed, and cared, and I have to accept that it was best. What is the right question? What if there's no answer?

The trains will continue to come. Who will keep the people on the platform?
I can only trust a few.

Did I wall you out, too, God? How do I let You in and, if I do, what will You do?
I don't know how to trust, or if I can, or if I want to try.

I hate the need of the wall; I fear its removal. It allows me to function; it keeps part of me locked in loneliness, sadness, and conflict.

I have a terrible secret.

CHAPTER 4 How to Move from Darkness into the Light

Shepherd of My Soul

Amy H.

The Lord is our Shepherd; He sees and knows all.
The wolf is here, in His house!
Dominating, condemning, shredding,
He confuses, horrifies, and injures.
Who will defend and save us?

The Shepherd watches—
perhaps He weeps—
as the sheep cringe in shock and respond in fear.
My soul hemorrhages in the awful silence;
I have not yet realized that I no longer breathe.

I stumble to the shadows, where my soul cowers still—
Unable to live, unable to die—
As darkness suffocates
And reason and hope fade.
Is there no one to depend on to defend and protect?

There are green pastures and quiet waters,
Yet, wounded and afraid, I will not be led.
I hide, withering and weeping alone.
And the Shepherd of my soul
Can only watch.

Hidden Place of Light

Lynne Head

There is a hidden room upstairs I fear
Therein lies the unknown terror to which I walk
A long dark corridor with doors closed
I fear one will open, and questions be posed.

The taunting of the enemy, the mockery the crime
I couldn't fight it off, my voice shut inside
the betrayal kept me silent, the powerlessness strong
to keep me from saying what will right the wrong

Something oh so cunning, something seeming
like an unseen spider's web, that trapped me inside.
I wanted to cry, but my heart went cold
standing left in shame which I cannot hide.

I want to kill the passion, stirred up inside of me
which left me feeling used, and my body burning hot.
I'd rather hate myself than to let myself again
ever want my heart to feel what it simply cannot.

I want to kill the longing which I didn't see.
How could one trick the tender part of me?
Yet with courage I continue to the darkened inner chamber,
like a haunted house, memories I wish not remember.

There is fear that terrifies and nightmares so true-
but somewhere deep inside me, I feel a candle burning.
There is more than this daunting hallway and fear that
   holds me back.
I must find the courage to learn the truth I'm yearning.

I feel a light shining, drawing me closer to Itself.
The terror doesn't take over me as much as I had thought.
Those screams and peals of laughter, mocking after me
are no longer gripping, are not reality.

There exists a true self somewhere deep within
saying His power is greater than all these awful things.
It's to Him I run now bravely and longing I embrace,
if I let it come alive, He will make me safe.

I've stepped over to th' other side, the door has opened wide,
the Light beams upon me brightly, it is Jesus I find.
He has brought His glory to shine upon my face.
There is no darkness 'round me, only light in this place.

Lead me Father, to Your side where I am not alone
to a place my heart's at rest, I may call it home.
Oh, I thank you Lord, for me your death,
has brought me to this Holy place of peace and rest.

I'm captive Holy Spirit, to live a life of with You;
when You enter, fill me, so my heart may find some comfort too.
I could have done this by myself, not with all my might,
So thank You Jesus for shining in the darkness with Your Light.

My Child, How Do You Feel?

Emily

Hopes and dreams crushed
Safety vanished
Confused and concerned
I feel heartbroken and sad.

Cast aside
He desired another
Left in fear of ever being genuinely loved
I feel betrayed, used, and unworthy.

Watching her pain
Frozen in fear
Not able to help
I feel useless and guilty.

Encouraged to play his game
Tricked and deceived
Forced to touch her
I feel manipulated and controlled.

Hearing her screams
Trying to comfort her
Offering comfort and a safe touch
I feel empathetic to her pain.

An adult walks in
Help at last
Instead an unloving stare, an awkward silence
I feel ashamed.

Helplessly waiting
Comfort not forthcoming
Emotions unprocessed
I feel overwhelmed and terrified.

Left in my pain
No one to turn to
Lonely and afraid
I feel abandoned and rejected.

Questions brewing
Open wounds festering
Unable to forget the pain
I feel wounded and hurt.

Is it safe to express my heart?
Will anyone listen?
Does anyone care?
I feel alone in my emotional pain.

Too scared to share
Afraid of rejection
Silenced - hold it all inside she implied
I feel voiceless.

A hatred of myself
Afraid of my feelings and desires
A hatred of the ones who hurt me
I feel angry and unkind.

Told it was all my fault
Told I was a horrible little girl
Told to keep it all a secret
I feel victimized and helpless.

My feelings are mine
No one can deny them
Only I can express them
I am learning to share my feelings.

CHAPTER 5 Why is Healthy Anger Necessary for Healing?

Sad, Angry, Afraid

Amy H.

Sad...
Helpless, hopeless, alone, overwhelmed, sobbing, filled with sorrow, despairing, wanting help but receiving none, grieving, heart-wrenching pain, unmet expectations, needy, abandoned, desperate then empty.

Angry...
Incredulity, confusion, searching, disappointment, horror, indignation, accusation, blame, frustration, rage, hate, refusal to love or trust, contempt, desire to strike, desire to yell/scream until I have no more breath or voice...guilt, shame, sorrow.

Afraid...
Who will help, vulnerable, small, unable to defend, untrusting, distant, hiding, no hope or expectation of help, unprotected, on my own, scared to receive help, lost, trapped.

CHAPTER 6 Broken Dreams

Dirty, Little Girl

Lynne Head

Dirty
little girl
sad
and torn
crying
inside
used
alone

soiled
and stained
running
home
for
dinner

could I
wash
and feel
better?

Secret
to keep
I'm so
ashamed

bound
to hate
my
desire

dirty
little girl
what have
I done?

I wrote this poem imagining God at the dinner table.

At My Father's Table

Lynne Head

Father:

Little girl, little girl
come take my hands
little girl oh, precious little girl
what has happened to You?

I can see your shame,
your eyes look afraid
and there is no laughter
on your face.

Little girl, precious girl
how I long to give
you my love
and endearing words.

But bring me your heart,
where have you put it?
You look so empty
without it.

Go and find it
and put it inside
for it is there I can put
my love and peace.

Take my hands
let me hold you tight
you want to be freed
from your pain.

Let me twirl you around
lift you up off the ground
let your spirit soar
with me.

Little Girl:

Oh Father, Father,
I am crying
for I have a pain
so deep

I've hidden my heart
because I felt so ashamed
I couldn't bear
to tell it.

I will take my heart
and entrust it to You
pray You will never
let it go.

For my fear is great.

Father:

Oh child, come to my table
where we can sit together
and be safe from any fear.
Stay with me, rest with me.

For in my Presence, my love is great.

CHAPTER 7 Grieving Lost Beauty

Fear of Beauty

Lynne Head

Why is it I so fear beauty?
For me, beauty stirs up evil.
But why can't beauty be strong?
Good?

For me- the memory of beauty
brings mocking, betrayal, deceit,
corruption, dishonesty, selfishness,
power plays, cheating,

something unwanted,
lack of trust,
sadness, fear, hopelessness,
godlessness.

When have I seen beauty good?
Give me an example.
It is only in Jesus I see
Faithful, trusting beauty that loves.

Everyone else has gone astray.
How my heart longs to be able
to trust in someone beautiful
who will not deceive me.

There is only one to trust.
One to lean on.
One to know.
One who will not turn on me.

Oh Jesus, teach me to hold on to You.
There must be a way to open up
my heart—if I can only learn to unfold
in the strength of Your love.

Though the storm shakes and
seeks to rattle me inside-
He longs to enter in and
calm the torrent of my soul.

Beauty is not bad, but so
many times it's played that way.
Where can I hear the music
of trust in a beautiful person?

I have a Man who lives inside me.
He is beauty itself. He has a
song He longs to sing if I
let Him open my heart to His tune.

Let it sing, let it trust. He can
conquer any evil or wrong.
It is so tender, yet so strong
in my heart—I want to surrender.

Beauty becomes a moment
of trust, a lifetime
of learning
what eternity is for.

When my heart can be
still and sing to Him,
beauty
will be good.

Resting in Beauty

Lynne Head

there is a fear
we have
of beauty

beauty is
a reflection
of God
but with it
are devil's
schemes

beauty fears
when
there
is
no trust
when
there
is
no good

beauty coils
in shame

longing
to be calm
everything's
going to be okay

the One who
made beauty
is by your side…
He made you
didn't He?

take a breath
let it shine
beauty
quietly
gracefully

if you can rest
it'll
make
you
weep
because
there
is
nothing
to
fear

CHAPTER 9 Holding onto Desire

Fear of Men

Lynne Head

Why do I fear men?
Cringing, looking away,
half-hearted conversation,
fear of fear itself-
all-consuming fire.

Young, innocent
turned dirty
dark.
Could terror,
trickery be restored?

Men cannot be trusted, there is not one-
my heart trusts no more.

In my heart
I know a Man who redeemed
the hearts of mankind.
A newfound hope
lies deep within.

His name is strong
His love true
Jesus, take my heart.
Steadfast.
You make new hearts of men.

Some can be trusted…
my heart believes in Him.

During my lunch break parked in front of a pond, I watched a grandfather feeding the ducks with his granddaughter. I reframed it little girl and her daddy.

Little Girl and Her Daddy

Lynne Head

He looks like my dad
gray hair, tanned skin
blue shirt.
She, a little curly
blonde.

He holds
her close
in his arms,
she's small
but he is strong.

They've come
to feed the ducks.
They waddle
they quack,
she laughs.

Then she falls
and cries
and he gathers
her up
comforting her.

He knows
her heart—
that's what it's
all
about.

CHAPTER 10 Is Jesus A Trustworthy Man?

I wrote about my anger. If I couldn't trust a Christian man, who could I trust?

Who is Jesus?

Lynne Head

Who is Jesus?
I ask
when my
heart
constricts
with
pain.

When I
suffer
with
grief
and
great
sorrow.

Tender
merciful,
fierce
with love,
He understands
like no
one else.

He doesn't
guilt or
shame,
He gently
leads me
back to
grace.

In
His arms,
holding me
His
heart
weeps
over me.

His kindness
heals
like cool water
for a thirsty
traveler,
like a gentle
rain..

Steady as
the ocean
wind,
He
gently
restores
my soul,

to
comfort
loss
and
heal
my
pain.

Who is Jesus?
He's the
missing
piece
that
makes me
whole.

To Be Safe

Lynne Head

I want to be safe
be at peace
and at ease

if this is
possible
I could
feel okay.

If I were
safe
then I
could trust,

I could
relax inside
and beauty
could open up.

I could
dance
and
breathe

I could laugh
jump
smile
learn

I could
enjoy life
around
me.

To be free.
Is this
the rest
He speaks of?

Resting in His
joy
resting in His
smile

I love to feel
His peace
and rest
awhile.

CHAPTER 11 Little Girls in Adult Bodies

Below are three poems. *Today* and *Little Girl* describe the heart of an emotionally dead person. *Innocence* describes the heart of an emotionally open person.

Today

Amy H.

A dead heart ...
and yet alive because it hurts.

A silent cry ...
to express a pain too great for words.

A distracted mind ...
to know and feel the loss again.

A secret moan ...
because my wounded soul still bleeds.

A stilled breath ...
to prove I cannot cope,
to stop the pain,
to cease to exist,
if only for a moment.

A verbal reprimand …
to subdue the needy part.

A dead heart.

Little Girl

Amy H.

You should be laughing, running through the flowers,
Instead you're cowering, alone with your tears.

You should be singing, dancing in the breezes,
Instead you're hiding, terrified to feel.

You should be safe, free to be alive,
Instead you've been crushed, betrayed, made to bleed.

You should know love, the hope of protection,
Instead you were abandoned, left alone to fend.

Fragile lady inside me, girl who's so sad,
Who did this? What happened…I don't understand.

Can you feel safe enough to tell your secrets? I'm so sorry…I don't
think I can bear to hear them all.

Darkness swirls in your heart—sorrow, pain, anger, shame, guilt, disappointment, hate, confusion, fear, despair, death.

You are me.
We do not laugh. We do not breathe. We do not feel. We do not trust. We do not love.
We do not live. We do not hope. We do not believe.

We hurt and we hide.

My body is rigid; my heart's made of stone.
Don't hurt me. Don't touch me. Don't help me. Don't love me.

Joy and peace are out of reach.
We won't be safe until we are Home.

Innocence

Emily

Hush, little child of mine
in my arms, in my arms
you will find love
love abiding, love unending
I give you my love.

Hush, little child of mine
in my arms, in my arms
you will find peace
peace indwelling
soothing your heart
I give you my peace.

Hush, little child of mine
in my arms, in my arms
you will find comfort
rest your weary head, upon my chest
in my presence, pain acknowledged
I give you my comfort.

Hush, little child of mine
in my arms, in my arms
you will find hope
bringing newness
restoring joy
I give you my hope.

Hush, innocent child of mine
in my arms, in my arms
you will find
One who sees, One who cares
One who judges rightly.
Hush, innocent child of mine, I love you!

CHAPTER 12 Becoming A Daughter

You Call Me Daughter

Amy H.

Known and loved,
    protected and nudged,
        desired and affirmed,
            You call me Daughter.

Chaos and calm,
    darkness and light,
        silence and song,
            You are my Father.

Hidden or present,
    fearful or strong,
        weary or joyful,
            You are my Father.

You call me.
    You call me.
        You call me
            Daughter.

From despair and darkness,
    from terror and death,
        from sin and self,
            You call me.

To joy and light,
    to truth and life,
        to holiness and love,
            You call me.

With tenderness and passion,
    with mercy and grace,
        with delight and longing,
            You call me.

Savior, Redeemer, Refuge, and King,
    You call me.
        You call me.
            You call me
                Daughter.

Princess Bride

Lynne Head

Today, I am a princess bride
wearing a crown of gold,
I smile with soft radiance.

Dressed in a gown
breath-taking
white.

No guilt
or stain.
Just free.

Not my strength
or power,
but Yours.

You shed
Your blood
for me.

Jesus clothes
me with
brilliance.

I know that I am
whole.

Ah, Lord Jesus
I bow
to You.

As I wait
for the Day
You fill my soul.

I
am
at peace.

Today,
I wear
this dress.

Tomorrow,
I can wear
it again.

Forever,
I'll wear
this gown.

For He's
washed
me.

I
am
pure.

What a
gracious
Bridegroom

And glorious
bride
I've become!

CHAPTER 13 Triggers and Trauma

Hardwood Floor

Lynne Head

Oft' times
I'm covered
like a carpet
on a floor.

I'm the floor
smothered
by a rug
holding
me down.

I can't breathe.

Oft' I allow
a man's presence
to oppress
like the rug.

I'm suffocating.

Wall to wall carpet
over plywood.
Powerless.

For too long
I shame myself
as inferior plywood.

Fear.
No life.
Little choice.

But I am
a hardwood floor,
not manmade.

Jesus created me.

I wrongly choose
to dip under
the rug of men.

They have no real
power over me,
but I let them
have it.

Like the dawning
of the day,
the Spirit
revealed to me.

I have found the answer.

Recondition.

It says in scripture
the veil tore in two.
Christ's death ripped
the carpet away.

It is time to be free;
to show the hardwood floor,
my value, my beauty.
Time to come out from hiding.

He is here.
Like the hardness of the floor,
so the hardness of the cross.

It wasn't a pleasant sight;
blood, broken flesh,
on a rugged piece of wood.

In exchange, He
cleanses, purifies.
I'm beautiful,
polished, smooth.

Why would I choose to hide?

He completed the work
once and for all.
He rolled up the carpet.
It's off.
I'm free.

Holding on at the End

Amy H.

I'm holding on,
here at the end of my rope.
I see now how I came to this place,
this point of weakness and despair,
of emptiness and vulnerability.
Apart from God, there is no meaning or purpose in life.
This conviction gives stability, but it also brings a tear.
God seems so far away sometimes.
My naked soul repulses me;
He is not surprised or offended by what He sees.
And so I hold on,
waiting,
for what or how long, I do not know.
The silence cuts my heart; my bleeding soul grows faint.
What am I to learn here at the end of my rope?
God is; He loves me; He is able.
He is all I need—is He all I desire?
Truth betrays knowledge.
Humbled and ashamed,
I weep.
God, if nothing else, help me not to let go.

CHAPTER 14 Learning Assertiveness

A Song

Lynne Head

Blue lines and feathers
black streaks with white
a pretty blue jay
sits in my sight.

He flits and flies
comes back again
oh what a treat
to look at him.

Music, beauty
color, and dance.
Deep inside he sings a song,
each bird God made takes a chance,
to Him they fly and they belong.

Created by Him, I have a song
I'm made to sing how I am free,
and share my joyful peaceful flight,
A beauty to share, a beauty to be.

Grant me grace to be myself and, enjoy who I am,
when I believe it's safe I'll fly
and bring all my glory to Him.

What colors shine in my life?
Do they dazzle, shimmer, and glisten?
Is it safe to offer what I long to share
to enjoy what's deep within?

O God, shine on me with Your grace
strengthen me to believe what You say is true
Open my heart and set me free—
to sing out my song to You.

Beginning to Believe

Lynne Head

I believe there's beauty inside, I have nothing at all to hide.
It's not what I weigh, not what I wear,
It's not my face, it's not my hair.

It's in my heart—that joy and peace,
freedom to shine
unafraid to receive.
For I know
there's beauty deep within,
From my maker, redeemer, friend in Him.

He gives rest unto my soul
A true purpose, making me whole.
He fills me up when I'm in need.
He's a safe place when I'm afraid.

He's given back my sense of worth
brought life in my rebirth.
Freedom I cry for release of my soul
believe in the One, let Him take control.

To the One I love, to the One who brought hope,
I'm finally believing that I can cope.
But in order to keep it I'll give it away.
Can't keep it locked up, for it to stay.

You're meant to release what's stored up inside,
life rises from death coming alive.
What's there in the heart is there to share,
there to give and love and care.

What is there now inside you to give?
Open the door, the longing will live,
you will unfold from the depths of your heart.
Don't be afraid or ashamed to start.

He's made you to give,
to enjoy being known.
Give it away,
you are not alone.

CHAPTER 15 When the Enemy Attacks

Out of the Shadows - Lovingly Exposed

Emily

Sitting in the shadows
overwhelming fear within
raging self-hatred engulfs me
punishment and condemnation await me
completely convinced is my heart

Sitting in the shadows
isolated and unknown
rejected and abandoned
hiding from the reach of others
blindly thinking this is safety and protection

Sitting in the shadows
alone with my shame, guilt, and tears
but not invisible, my Heavenly Father saw and knew every detail
He understood my deepest heart's desire and fear that day
to come and cry freely in His loving arms

Out of the shadows
seen and accepted
known and unconditionally loved
through His blood - a costly price-
clothed in His righteousness am I

Out of the shadows
consuming fear of my past no longer wages war in my soul
hiding no part of my heart in the shadows, peace indwells
free to be me, free to be whole
walking in the light of His love

Out of the shadows
dignity and worth secure in Him,
freely loving others birthed
forgiving and receiving forgiveness
knowing His blood was shed for All

Some days doubt and fear anew
some days again to the shadows I flee
but daily hope comes forth through trust and dependence
    on HIM
gently exposing my heart, leading me out of the shadows
into His loving arms

Why would I choose
sitting in the shadows,
when I know there is freedom
in the loving exposure of truth and light
living outside the shadows?

CHAPTER 16 Finding Forgiveness

She Didn't Protect Me

Lynne Head

I didn't understand it then
but now it's all so clear
when I entered into their home
she didn't want me there.

She must have felt rejected
or thought *he's done it again*
quietly she stood and suffered
speaking not a word to him.

She could have said, "don't do that
I see your secret war,
there's something so much better
that your life could stand for."

I'm angry with this woman
for in her silent way
he abused my body
struck, downcast I lay.

I've harbored intense hatred
against their selfish sin,
my body scorned the hand
from shameful deeds of man.

Wanting to scream out loud,
wishing I could cry
to reveal their evil schemes
so that I wouldn't die.

I could never find the justice
to condemn them both to death
I have no power of my own,
so why not save my breath?

I must trust the God the Father
as terrible as this was,
for His love and mercy
always coming from above.

I must let go of wanting
to seek revenge myself
open up my hands and heart
and cry to Him for help.

Marked

Emily

Marked by debilitating shame, I hide
wondering did I cause this
my desire, her deepest pain
Who am I?

Marked by ravishing guilt, I blame
anger and resentment, fear and unbelief
my companions leaving me to die
Who am I?

Marked by deepest doubt, I fear
love will never reach my heart
piercing wails, excruciating pain
Who am I?

Marked by Satan's lies, I weep
too tired, too weary to resist
too scared, too stubborn to ask for help
Who am I?

Marked by dependence on another, I trust
bloodied hands, feet, and side - wonderful Jesus
lovingly marked by God, willingly died, His wrath satisfied
Jesus, who am I?

Marked by something better
allowing me to live by faith
secure in Him
This is who I am

Marked by brokenness, I rest
trusting in His sovereign plan
even when I do not understand
This is who I am

Marked by love, I forgive
releasing others, releasing myself
into the Potter's holy hands
This is who I am

Marked by courage, I walk
letting God use me in His perfect way
now vulnerable and transparent my heart
This is who I am

Marked by compassion, I speak
of life experiences, allowed by Him
proclaiming His goodness, His redeeming love
This is who I am

Who am I?
marked am I
marked by my past
marked by my God

Who am I?
marked am I
marked by God's love, His purpose to reveal
marked by my Savior, His glory to reveal

CHAPTER 17 Transforming Shame

*P*ure

Emily

Longings slowly rise
giving way to
passion ignited, love desired

Willingly I surrender
sensing the pleasure
in His loving touch

No fear of shame
no fear of blame
past memories no longer taint

Living in the moment
deeply known, completely loved
desired and enjoyed

Dignity and worth restored
in the choosing of love
His and mine to decide

Intimate and close
partaking in each other
body and soul satisfied

Purest desire
love not taken
nor demanded

Purest joy
love gladly given
and freely received

Purest love
sacred and special
right and good

Creator of Woman

Lynne Head

He is the Master, the One
who made me woman.
I live in my body, but it is
He who created it.

Just what does it mean
to be a woman?
How does it feel
when I am woman?

Like a bird spreading
its wings,
letting go,
not afraid to fly.

Safe in my flight
secure from harm.
This is what gives me
permission to release.

Give away what's inside
a tender place
I long to fill others
with warmth and love.

That's what it's like
soaring above
creative and fun,
a smile on my face

hands opened up
this is when life
is worth living for me,
being a woman in love.

In love by my Master,
He's created me
to give of myself
because He died for me.

With a man like that
who touches my heart,
I cannot stop what flows inside.
Let it never, never end.

He touches the deepest place.
If I could linger forever here,
my heart would keep going
like mountain waters falling,

Jesus touch me inside
Your constant love flowing.
I'm blessed You
made me a woman.

CHAPTER 18 Developing Closeness

Jesus, Lover of my Soul

Lynne Head

It matters to You when I cry.
Jesus, take my face in Your hands
touch my cheeks with Your fingers.
look me in the eyes.

We are in love-
me and You.
You melt my heart,
Oh Jesus, rapture me.

Your manly strength
surrounds me
with warmth and safety
I've never known.

Jesus, You kiss me
and speak tenderly.
Stroke my hair—
take Your hand in mine.

CHAPTER 19 Longing for A Safe Place

Rider
(Rev 19: 11-16)

Lynne Head

You, the Rider standing there
dressed in garments dipped
in Your blood.

You've done the deed,
Done the necessary.
The price, your life.

You ride to fight,
crowned with many crowns
displaying past victories.

Your eyes shine like blazing fire
a sharp sword
between your teeth.

They call You Faithful and True
written upon you, a powerful name
no one knows.

The beating drum announces
just behind riders,
dressed in white for battle.

This is not sweet fellowship.
Not time for love,
NOW's a time of war.

I taste your great authority,
on your robe
and thigh is written:

KING OF KINGS,
AND LORD OF LORDS.

Who can stand against
or defy your holy name?
The beast and kings
of earth are doomed.

The Word of God is here.
The time comes for justice,
when He will right all wrong.

He is patient,
some thought He'd never come.
The white horse is here.

The Rider is on His way.

Would I?

Lynne Head

If I were in heaven
Would I see You in Your glory?
Would I stand by the crystal sea?
Would I cry Holy, Holy, Holy?

Would I lay my crown at Your feet?
Would I fall before the lamb, and play a harp of gold?
Would my prayers offer sweet fragrance to the King?
Would I hear the angels sing, Oh my soul!

Would I see people from every tribe and language?
And kneel with every person in heaven and on earth
Singing to the Lamb of God,
The highest One of worth.

If I were in heaven
Yes, I'd cry Holy, Holy, Holy!
And I would sing worthy!
I would be filled with Your glory.

If I were in heaven
I would see the Lord's beauty and love,
I would fall upon my face and sing
To the One who reigns above.

References

Page 18:
Langberg, D.M. (1999). *On the Threshold of Hope* (L. Vanderzalm, Ed).

Page 21:
Child Safety & Protection Network, *Best Practice Standards for Missions Agency Child Safety Policies and Procedures*, (2013, September 10), p. 5.

Child Safety & Protection Network, *Best Practice Standards for Missions Agency Child Safety Policies and Procedures*, (2013, September 10), p. 6.

Child Safety & Protection Network, *Introduction and Background*, (2013, September 10), p. 5.

Page 39:
Brussels lace. (2022). Retrieved March 11, 2022, from https://en.wikipedia.org

Page 54:
Coe, J. H. (2015). "Anger, Prayer, and the Imprecatory Psalms in Relation to Mental Health," Talbot School of Theology.

Page 89:
Roberto, M (2021, February 25). *Rose McGowan backs Cuomo accuser Lindsey Boylan, calls for investigation into 'monstrous' claims*. Retrieved from http://www.foxnews.com

Almukhtar, S. Gold, M. Buchanan, L. (2018, February 8). *After Weinstein: 71 Men Accused of Sexual Misconduct and Their Fall From Power* Retrieved from http://www.nytimes.com

Los Angeles Times Staff (2021, June 30). *Timeline of Bill Cosby sexual assault scandal: Full coverage of allegations, trial*. Retrieved from http://www.latimes.com

Rhodes, J. (2020, August 10). *What Did Jeffrey Epstein Do? Look Back at His Crimes and Charges 1 Year After His Death*. Retrieved from http://www.intouchweekly.com/posts/what-did-jeffrey...

Ethics Unwrapped. Penn State Scandal.
Retrieved from http://www.ethicsunwrapped.utexas.edu/video/penn-state-scandal

Murphy, D. Barr, J. (2021, February 25). *Ex-USA Gymnastics coach John Geddert kills himself after felony charges, including human trafficking, sexual assault*. Retrieved from http://www.espn.com

Page 90:
Quotes Sign (2022). *57 Trust Broken Quotes, Captions & Images Free Download*.[Web blog post]. Retrieved February 4, 2022 from https://quotessign.com

Page 102:
Seifert, K (2014, February 18). *Death by Stoning: Why Is This Sickening Punishment Legal?* [Web blog post]. Retrieved March 17, 2019 from https://www.psychologytoday.com

Page 109-110:
Sutherland, Dr. C. (2022) *Letters to my Brown Girls,* Publish Your Gift.

Page 111:
Wessell, W. (1984) Mark. In F. E. Gaebelein (Ed.), The Expositor's Bible Commentary (Vol. 8, 660-664). ZondervanPublishingHouse

Page 131:
NIMH (last revised 2019, May) *Post-Traumatic Stress Disorder.* Retrieved from https://www.nimh.nih.gov

Page 132:
Wlassoff, V. (2015, January 24). How does post-traumatic stress disorder change the brain? [Neuroscience a d Neurology]. Retrieved August 30, 2019, from http://brainblogger.com.

Wlassoff, V. (2015, January 24). How does post-traumatic stress disorder change the brain? [Neuroscience a d Neurology]. Retrieved August 30, 2019, from http://brainblogger.com

Debiec, J. (2018, September 24). Memories of trauma are unique because of how brains and bodies respond to threat [Psychology and Psychiatry]. Retrieved from http://medicalxpress.com

Page 133:
ScienceDaily (2018, December 10). *Your brain on imagination: It's a lot like reality, study shows.* Retrieved from www.sciencedaily.com/releases/2018/12/181210144943.htm

Page 135:
Victim (n.d.) In *Oxford Advanced Learner's Dictionary.* Retrieved from https://www.oxfordlearnersdictionaries.com

Page 187:
Burke, J. (2015). *Imagine Heaven.* Baker Books.

About the Author

Lynne Head is a licensed clinical mental health counselor. She received her MS in counseling at Cairn University and her MA in Christian Education from Columbia International University. Lynne has experience in behavioral health counseling with several agencies and currently maintains a private counseling practice. She and her husband served in France as church planters and counsel with World Team, a global mission organization.

At twenty-two, Lynne received counseling after surviving a car accident and death of a close friend. Through the grief process, she formed an interest in counseling. Many years later, Lynne lost her 16-year-old son tragically in a car accident which caused significant health issues. These experiences have given Lynne a sensitivity to those who experience tragedy, grief, and chronic pain. Her experience as a pastor's wife and a missionary have given her a desire to create a safe place for others in ministry in the states and overseas.

Learn more about Lynne's counseling practice and writing at www.lynnehead.com. She writes monthly devotionals for VineWords.

Lynne lives with her husband, Jim in Charlotte. She has two adult daughters, five grandchildren, and one son in heaven.

Printed in the USA
CPSIA information can be obtained
at www.ICGtesting.com
JSHW021102281123
52546JS00004B/14

9 781614 938866